READY-TO-USE
ACTIVITIES AND MATERIALS ON
COASTAL
INDIANS

A Complete Sourcebook
for Teachers K-8

DANA NEWMANN

NATIVE AMERICANS RESOURCE LIBRARY

**THE CENTER FOR APPLIED
RESEARCH IN EDUCATION**
West Nyack, New York 10994

Library of Congress Cataloging-in-Publication Data

Newmann, Dana.
  Ready-to-use activities and materials on Coastal Indians :
a complete sourcebook for teachers K-8 / Dana Newmann.
      p.   cm.—(Native Americans resource library : unit 3)
  Includes bibliographical references.
  ISBN 0-87628-609-0 (pbk.)
    1. Indians of North America—Pacific coast (North America)
2. Indian craft. I. Title. II. Series: Newmann, Dana. Native American resource library ; v. 3.
  E76.6.N48 1997 vol. 3
  [E78.P2]
  978'.00497 s—dc20   96-35340
  [372.89]   CIP

©1996 by The Center for Applied Research in Education

Every effort has been made to ensure that no copyrighted material has been used without permission. The author regrets any oversights that may have occurred and would be happy to rectify them in future printings of this book.

Printed in the United States of America

10 9 8 7 6 5 4 3 2 1

ISBN 0-87628-609-0

ATTENTION: CORPORATIONS AND SCHOOLS

Prentice Hall books are available at quantity discounts with bulk purchase for educational, business, or sales promotional use. For information, please write to: Prentice Hall Career & Personal Development Special Sales, 113 Sylvan Avenue, Englewood Cliffs, NJ 07632. Please supply: title of book, ISBN number, quantity, how the book will be used, date needed.

**THE CENTER FOR APPLIED RESEARCH
IN EDUCATION**
West Nyack, NY 10994
A Simon & Schuster Company

On the World Wide Web at http://www.phdirect.com

Prentice Hall International (UK) Limited, *London*
Prentice Hall of Australia Pty. Limited, *Sydney*
Prentice Hall Canada, Inc., *Toronto*
Prentice Hall Hispanoamericana, S.A., *Mexico*
Prentice Hall of India Private Limited, *New Delhi*
Prentice Hall of Japan, Inc., *Tokyo*
Simon & Schuster Asia Pte. Ltd., *Singapore*
Editora Prentice Hall do Brasil, Ltda., *Rio de Janeiro*

¡ MIL GRÁCIAS, E.N.!

ABOUT THE AUTHOR

A graduate of Mills College in Oakland, California, Dana Newmann has been an elementary teacher for more than 15 years. She has taught in California and New Mexico and for the U.S. Army Dependents Group in Hanau, Germany.

Mrs. Newmann has authored a variety of practical aids for teachers, including *The New Teacher's Almanack* (The Center, 1980), *The Early Childhood Teacher's Almanack* (The Center, 1984), and *The Complete Teacher's Almanack* (The Center, 1991).

She presently lives in Santa Fe, New Mexico, where for the past seven years she has worked for Project Crossroads, a nonprofit educational resource organization. Mrs. Newmann heads the elementary school program and conducts workshops for teachers throughout the state and the Southwest.

ABOUT THE NATIVE AMERICAN REVIEWER OF THIS BOOK

Margaret Adams, whose father was Native American, lives on the Monterey Peninsula in California.

She holds two B.A. degrees in Anthropology, and in Art History as well as a Master's degree in Anthropology from the University of Pittsburgh. Ms. Adams has worked in several museums, including the Utah State Museum and the De Young Museum, Indian Arts Department in San Francisco. Ms. Adams has been personally connected with the Hupa tribe for decades.

A FEW WORDS ABOUT THE NATIVE AMERICANS RESOURCE LIBRARY

The *Native Americans Resource Library* is a four-book series that introduces you and your students in grades K-8 to the lives of the peoples who have inhabited North America for thousands of years. The four books in this Resource Library are:

- Ready-to-Use Activities and Materials on *Desert Indians (Unit I)*
- Ready-to-Use Activities and Materials on *Plains Indians (Unit II)*
- Ready-to-Use Activities and Materials on *Coastal Indians (Unit III)*
- Ready-to-Use Activities and Materials on *Woodland Indians (Unit IV)*

Each unit in the series is divided into the following sections:

- "Their History and Their Culture"—Here you'll find information about the historical background of the particular region ... food ... clothing ... shelter ... tools ... language ... arts and crafts ... children and play ... religion and beliefs ... trade ... social groups and government ... when the Europeans came ... the native peoples today ... Historic Native Americans of the particular region.

- "Activities for the Classroom"—Dozens of meaningful activities are described to involve your students in creating and exploring with common classroom materials: native shelters, tools, jewelry, looms; also included are directions for making and playing traditional Native American games; foods of the particular region ... and *much* more!

- "Ready-to-Use Reproducible Activities"—These are 45 full-page worksheets and activity sheets that can be duplicated for your students as many times as needed. The reproducible activities reinforce in playful and engaging ways the information your student have learned about a particular region.

- "Teacher's Resource Guide"—You'll find lists of catalogs, activity guides, professional books, and children's books covering the specific region you're studying.

Throughout each book in the series are hundreds of line drawings to help illustrate the information. A special feature of each book are the many historic photographs that will help "bring to life" the Native American tribes as they were in the 19th and early 20th centuries!

The *Native Americans Resource Library* is designed to acquaint you and your students with this important and complex subject in a direct *and* entertaining way, encouraging understanding and respect for those people who are the *first* Americans.

CONTENTS

THE COASTAL INDIANS: THEIR HISTORY AND THEIR CULTURE
1

THE COASTAL INDIANS: ACTIVITIES FOR THE CLASSROOM 167

THE COASTAL INDIANS:
READY-TO-USE REPRODUCIBLE ACTIVITIES
201

THE COASTAL INDIANS: TEACHER'S RESOURCE GUIDE
251

A NOTE FROM THE AUTHOR ABOUT THIS BOOK

The first settlers of this continent have been known traditionally as American Indians. In recent years many people have come to think this term is inaccurate, based as it is on Christopher Columbus's mistaken idea that he had arrived at islands off of India. Today some descendants of those original settlers still use the term American Indian, while others prefer to define themselves as Native Americans, or First Americans. Furthermore, the Eskimo-Aleut peoples of the Arctic region—whose ancestors crossed over the Bering Strait thousands of years after the original migrations—are often referred to separately as Native Alaskans.

In the pages that follow we will look at the lives of those early Americans who settled the present-day states of California, Oregon, Washington, and Alaska: how they may have arrived there, and how they organized their lives during the centuries since then. Next we will consider the effects on these peoples of the arrival of the Europeans and, last, we will look at the contemporary life of those who today live in this vast and diverse area.

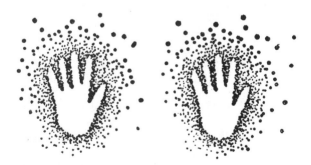

Today it is essential that students realize that their way of life is not solely the creation of twentieth-century people. Much that is beautiful and that enriches our museums, our libraries and—potentially—our lives, has been given to us by the first inhabitants of the Pacific Coast states. Our children should understand this; this book will show you and your students the specific gifts we have received from these early Americans.

Native American cultures teach each person to have respect for all living things, emphasizing what it means to live in harmony with one's surroundings; they show that every action in the natural world has consequences. These are essential lessons for each of us to understand—and to teach—as we enter the twenty-first century.

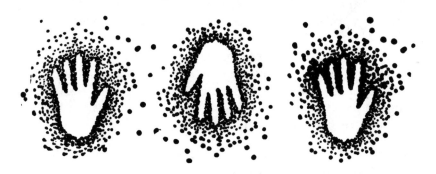

It has been my intent to write clearly and simply, so that even young children may understand a very complex subject; these pages offer only a first glimpse into a vastly fertile and unique area of study. It is my hope that this book will be just the beginning for you and your students in your explorations into Native American studies—together!

Dana Newmann

THE
COASTAL INDIANS

Their History
and Their Culture

PREHISTORY AND GEOGRAPHY

Archaeologists say that some 25,000 years ago—toward the end of the last glaciers—people moved across the Bering Strait, which was then a land bridge. Those early people were probably searching for food and following the tracks of woolly mammoths or saber-tooth tigers. Eventually they walked the 55 miles from Siberia to Alaska—and became the very first North Americans![1]

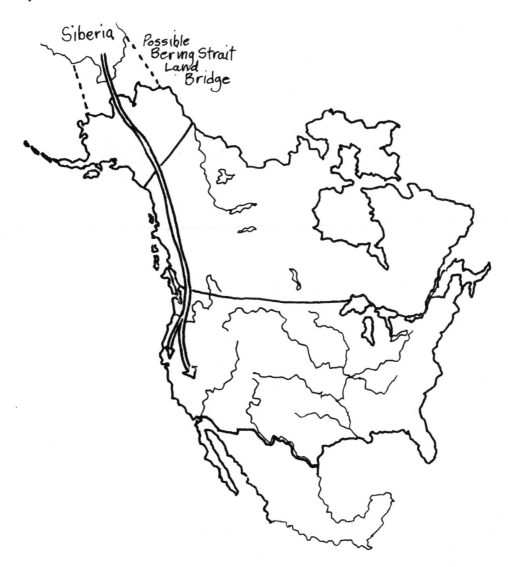

As the Ice Age ended, about 10,000 years ago, the weather and geography of North America changed—and the big game vanished. In parts of the West the old hunting tribes gave way to bands, small groups of families, that moved with the seasons in search of food. They set up camps where they hunted small animals, fished, or gathered wild plants and seeds.

In California the acorn of the oak tree became the main food. People learned how to grind the acorn into flour, which made it possible to carry a food supply as they traveled between the oak groves and their hunting grounds. As time went on and trade developed, many of the bands in California settled into village life.

Fish was the main food source in the Pacific Northwest, where many streams and rivers flow from the Cascade Mountains to the sea. Some of the big rivers, like the Columbia, were used to travel between the inland Plateau and the coast, which was settled by people who ate shellfish and hunted sea animals.

The sea-going Eskimo-Aleuts were the last to come over from Asia, in about 3000 B.C. There was no longer a land bridge between Siberia and Alaska so they crossed the Bering Strait in wooden or skin boats, or rode in on floating ice. Those who settled on the coasts of northern and western Alaska hunted sea animals and migrating caribou.

By the time Christopher Columbus arrived at this continent, there were hundreds of thousands of Native Americans living in what are now the coastal states of California, Oregon, Washington, and Alaska. The culture areas of these peoples—based on ancestry, climate, and geography—do not fall neatly within state lines.

The coastal peoples lived from the sea to the mountain ranges that run parallel to it. Some of them lived quite far away from the ocean, and may have never seen it, but their way of life was connected to the sea by custom, climate, vegetation, rivers, trade routes, and by family ties to peoples who lived on the coast.

There were fewer people in the inland areas east of the mountains. The climate was generally drier and harsher and the groups that lived there were more like their neighbors to the east.

CALIFORNIA

The early Native Americans of California came from several tribal groups and spread out into California's many life zones. Each of these life zones has a certain climate with particular animals and plants; as people moved into them, they based their daily lives on their natural surroundings.

By A.D. 300 most Californians lived in villages made up of related families. Each village (or small group of villages) ruled itself and had little to do with its neighbors—or

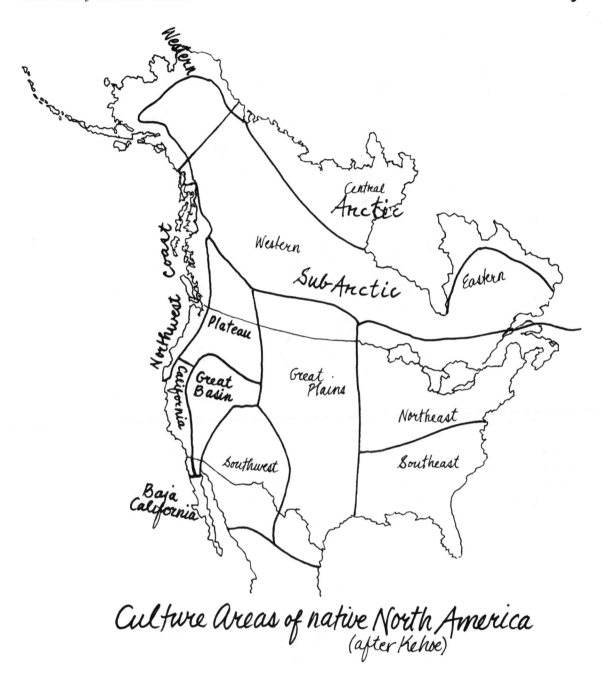

Culture Areas of native North America
(after Kehoe)

even with its old tribal group. When the Spanish came, they found more than 60 languages (and over 300 dialects!) being spoken in California.

Most early California people did not have to spend much time making clothes or shelters because the climate was mild. There was plenty of water, animal life, and a wide variety of seed-bearing plants. Because of this, California had more early people living in it than were found in any other area of the continent north of Mexico!

The California culture area included most of the state except for the lands east of the Sierra Nevada and a few places on the border with Oregon.

Life Zones of California
(after Faber-Lasagna)
High Mountains ●
Mountainous ◓
Foothills ◍
Valley and Desert ○

East of the Sierra Nevada

The Mojave and other Colorado River peoples lived on the flood plains of that river and in the hot and barren lands around it. They were related to Southwest culture people who lived nearby in Mexico and Arizona.

People from the Great Basin culture area, relatives of the Paiutes and the Western Shoshoni, lived on the eastern slopes of the Sierra and down to the desert below it.

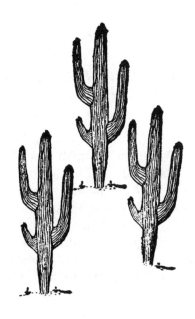

Southern California

In southern California there are coastal areas, deserts, valleys, foothills, and a scattering of mountains. Most of the area is hot and dry, but there are lakes, streams, and water holes scattered throughout it.

The so-called Mission Indians[2] (Luiseño, Cupeño, Gabrielino, Cahuilla, and others) lived near the Mexican border and along the foothills.

The coastal Chumash lived near present-day Santa Barbara. They built boats and their camps have been found out on the Channel Islands.

Central California

In central California is the Great Central Valley with its rivers, grass, marshlands, and wooded areas. This was home to the Salinan, Yokut, and Costanoan peoples.

As we move north we find more rivers, many flowing together into San Francisco Bay. The San Joaquin and Sacramento rivers meet to form a natural basin where the North Valley Yokut, Miwok, and southern Maidu (or Nissenan) lived.

The Esselen, Coast Miwok, Yuki, Pomo, and others lived near the California coastline, where seafood was plentiful.

Northern California

What we may call the Native California way of life ended around Cape Mendocino. North of there lived the Shasta, Yurok, Hupa, and Karuk; their way of life was more like that of their neighbors to the north and east.

OREGON AND WASHINGTON

The many groups that make up the Northwest Coast culture lived by the Pacific coast (and on the offshore islands) from Cape Mendocino to southern Alaska. Much of this area is wooded and not so cold as you might think. It is protected from the freezing Arctic air by mountain ranges and the land is warmed by moist breezes from the North Pacific. The nearby Japanese current brings gentle soft rains to northern California, heavy rains to Oregon and Washington, and downpours to Juneau.

The oceans, rivers, and forests of Oregon and Washington gave the people much fish and game. It is said that they could have survived on just the salmon supply.[3] The wood from the forests was used to make large houses (built without nails), water-tight boxes, and excellent sea-going boats.

When the Europeans arrived, they found many settlements in the coastal areas. Some of the better-known groups living there at that time were the Tillamook, Coast Salish, and Makah.

People who spoke Chinook languages lived along the Columbia River from the coast up to Dalles Falls, where the river breaks out from the Columbia Plateau. A trading language, Chinook Jargon or Chinook Wawa, was used by travelers and traders in this area.

Most of the inland Indians of Oregon and Washington lived on the Columbia Plateau and the eastern slopes of the Cascade Range, where their lives were centered on the many rivers that provided food and routes of trade and travel.

The Plateau Indians included the Modoc, Klamath, Walla Walla, and Nez Perce of central and northeast Oregon, and the Spokane, Yakima, and Columbia peoples of eastern Washington.

The Northern Paiute lived in the desert lands of eastern Oregon.

ALASKA

For eight months of the year most of Alaska is covered with snow; winds blow, piling up huge snow drifts and leaving the rocks and crags bare. During a brief summer, the tundra (rocky open plains) is covered with tiny wildflowers, and the sun never sets.

The Haida and Tlingit settled in the warmer part of Alaska, on the southern coasts and wooded islands. They are related by language to the inland Athapaskans, but their way of life is like that of the Northwest Coast peoples.

Much of inland Alaska, where temperatures can range from -80° F. to +100° F., is *taiga,* forests of fir trees. The Athapaskan-speaking Indians who settled this area led nomadic lives, following the seasons, traveling by foot and on snowshoes, pulling their sleds by hand and using their dogs as pack animals.

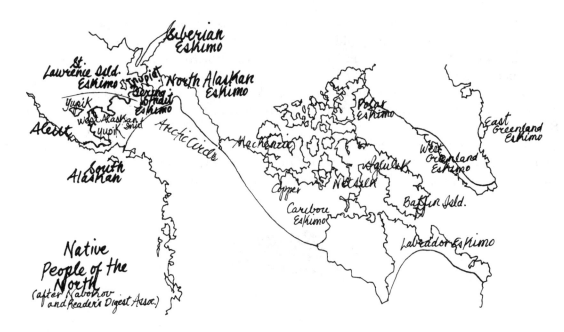

Eskaleuts

The ancestors of the Eskimos and Aleuts settled the coastal tundra of Alaska and the islands that stretch out towards Siberia.

Inuits/Eskimos[4]   The Inuit/Eskimo culture area stretches all the way from Siberia to Greenland. The Alaskan Inuits can be divided into two main culture and language groups, one speaking Yupik and the other Inupiat.

Coming home, baby in sled; baby in parka; boy runs ahead.

Yupiks   The Yupiks, also known as South Alaskan Eskimo (or Pacific Inuits), settled mostly on the tundra along the Pacific coast of Alaska where the waters do not freeze solid; this made it possible to hunt sea animals from boats most of the year.

Sea hunting in winter

Inupiats   The Inupiats (also known as the North Alaska Eskimo) are found along the coast from Norton Sound north. This is the area where the basic Eskimo way of life is thought to have begun. In these Arctic regions there is little or no wood and the sea freezes over in winter, making it impossible to hunt with boats.

Earth-covered houses
Man skinning reindeer
Frozen Sea

Aleuts   The Aleut (Al-OOt) people, distant relatives of the Inuits, settled the Alaskan peninsula west of Port Moller and the volcanic islands that mark the boundary between the Pacific Ocean and the Bering Sea. Like the Northwest Coast people, they built timbered houses.

Coming home to a earth-covered house: Inuit

The early Alaskan peoples lived mainly in small extended family groups and counted on each other, within their groups, to keep themselves alive. Life in these lands was dangerous and risky and *people,* not things, were the most valuable resource.

Notes for "Prehistory and Geography":

1. This is the common understanding of anthropologists but is not accepted by some Native Americans, who rely on their creation legends to explain their presence on this continent. Even scientists disagree about the first crossing. Some would date it back to 50,000 years ago.
2. Spanish missions were established in California from 1769 on. Indian groups were given names like Juanino and Gabrielino, referring to the names of missions nearby. Today, some of these peoples have taken back their native names.
3. As the glaciers melted, the sea levels rose and changed the coastline. The great annual spawning runs of the Pacific salmon didn't settle into their modern pattern until about 2000 B.C.
4. It has been thought that "Eskimo" comes from the Algonquian word *eskimantik,* eaters of raw flesh; this is how they were seen by the inland people. Later the Europeans adopted this name for them, even though these coastal hunters called themselves "Inuit," which means "the people" in their own language. Today many of these people prefer to be known as Inuit.

FOOD

All people, in all cultures, have the same basic needs: food to nurture their bodies, and clothing and shelter to protect them from extreme heat, cold, and rain.

So it was with the early Native American, also.

CALIFORNIA

The early men of California hunted for deer, small animals, birds and fish; the women either roasted the meat (to be eaten at once), or dried and stored it for winter.

The women and girls gathered young bulbs and tender plants in spring, and seeds and berries during the summer. Acorns, fruits, and nuts were gathered in the fall. Then, all winter, they lived on the foods they had stored.

Native Californians traded for salt, pine nuts, and (dried) seafood—depending on where they each lived and what they needed.

There are signs that the Colorado River people grew squash and pumpkins in fields that were watered by the river. The harvested vegetables were boiled or roasted and the pumpkin seeds were sundried.

Plants

Acorns   The acorn, which is the seed of the oak tree, was the main food of California Indians. Acorns are rich in sugar, starch, and citric acid. The oaks drop their acorns twice each autumn. The first batch that falls is usually full of worms, so the early people left this on the ground to be eaten by squirrels and other small animals. It was the second batch that was gathered for food.

Gathering   The California Indians often honored the arrival of the acorn-gathering season with a special ceremony.[1] (See **Religion and Beliefs**.)

The women and children gathered the acorns and put them into large burden baskets. (See **Tools and Gear**.) They worked hard, as it took a whole day to harvest one tree—which could give up to 140 pounds of acorns![2]

Drying and Storing   The acorns were spread out on flat rocks or mats and left to dry in the sun for a few weeks.

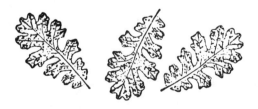

Preparation   Each dried acorn was shelled by tapping it firmly with a hammer stone. (See **Tools and Gear**.) Next, the nuts were put in a winnowing basket to separate the husks from the kernels, which were then ground with a mortar and pestle. These steps took a very long time. (See Photo 1.)

Acorns have an extremely bitter taste because they contain tannic acid. Before acorn meal could be cooked and eaten, it was necessary to remove the acid and its bad taste by a process called "leaching," which *also* took a long time.[3]

Photo 1. Mono women with baskets for acorn meal. *Courtesy San Diego Museum of Man.*

Cooking   Cereals, breads, and soups were prepared from acorn meal by mixing it with fresh water in a cooking basket. Next, clean hot stones were dropped into the basket to cook the cereal. (See **Tools and Gear**.)

The Mojave and Chumash cooked their acorn mush right over the fire in pottery or soapstone (steatite) bowls.

Agave (ah-GAH-vay)   The agave (mescal, or century plant) was used by the southern California Indians for food. They boiled the flower for a few minutes to take out the bitterness and ate the blossoms, or stored them for up to five years!

Mesquite (mes-KEET) Southern California tribes roasted mesquite flowers in a pit with heated stones and then squeezed them into little balls, which they then stored. When needed, the preserved mesquite balls were cooked in boiling water.

The green bean pods were boiled for eating, or crushed and soaked in water to make a refreshing drink. They could also be dried and pounded into meal that was then made into little cakes and stored to become a fine trail food!

Pine Nuts These tiny seeds, rich in protein and fat, were enjoyed by all the early California people. Pine nuts were eaten raw, boiled into a mush, or pounded and made into small cakes.

Other Edible Plants The early Californians used *many* other plants for food, including yucca, camas lily, cattails, wild onions, wild grapes, and wild berries.

Meat

Game The men hunted rabbits, squirrels, desert sheep, deer, antelope, and elk. Most tribes would not eat bear[4]; and some tribes would not eat coyote, gray fox, marten, or frogs.

Fowl Marine and freshwater birds and also quail, pigeon and doves were hunted with bows and arrows, nets, snares, slings, clubs, and baskets. Seabird eggs, a rich source of protein, were prized. There were birds which, for reasons of religion or taste, certain tribes would not eat; these included buzzard, magpie, crow, and eagle.

Fish In the many lakes and rivers, the early people caught trout, bass, salmon, perch, catfish, sturgeon, and eel.

Seafood Those who lived near the ocean ate many kinds of seafood: abalone, mussels, clams, barnacles, oysters, crabs, sea urchins, snails, chiton, and octopus. The fish they caught included sea bass and salmon.

Early Californians did not go out to hunt whales, but if one washed up on the beach the people rejoiced—and then roasted and ate the meat. Extra whale meat was cut into strips and dried for later use.

Seabirds Coastal Californians ate seabirds: cranes, pelicans, herons, cormorants, seagulls, and terns. The Costanoan, Salinan, and Esselen peoples loved cormorant eggs and, at certain times of the year, they would take boats to offshore islands to gather them.

OREGON AND WASHINGTON

The Northwest people were mainly meat and fish eaters. There was plenty of game in the forests, but hunting was hard because of the rugged ground and thick plant growth. Fishing and sea hunting were also rich sources of food.

People in this area cooked their food by grilling, baking, boiling, or, as with clams, by steaming.[5]

Meat

Fish   From the sea and rivers the early people got many kinds of fish: herring, smelt, salmon,[6] and olachen (eulachon or candlefish). Olachen is an extremely oily fish that cannot be dried, so it was pressed to drain off its oil which was then used as a sauce at special feasts.

Fish Eggs   The coastal people set rows of fir branches, which were held under water by rocks, in places where they knew the herring spawned. After the herring laid down its large sticky mass of eggs, the people simply pulled up the branches—eggs and all.

Fish eggs, called roe, were eaten fresh or dried for later use.

Shellfish   Shellfish, including mussels and clams, were found all along the coastline and were easy to collect. How do we know that the early people of this region ate lots of shellfish? Because we have found the huge piles of shells they left beside their coastal villages!

Whales and Other Sea Mammals   Seals, sea lions, porpoises, and sea otters, when available, were hunted and eaten by some coastal groups in the Northwest.

Only a few of these early people went whaling. They ate and dried as much of the meat as they could, but it was the whale *oil*, taken from the outside layer of fat (blubber), that they most wanted!

The women would cut off the fat from any dead whales that drifted ashore. Oils were very important to people who didn't have much starch or sugar to eat.

Game   Depending on what animals were available, the hunters of the Northwest would work singly or in groups, with or without the help of dogs. They used spring poles, snares, pitfalls, or bow and arrow. Land hunting, however, was not so important to these people as sea and river hunting.

Plants

There were few plants to eat except for the edible bulb of the camas lily (found in the southern inlands), acorns (to the far south), and the many berries.

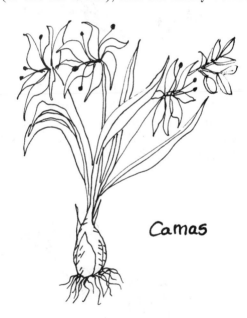

Camas

The tough stringy roots of some ferns, one kind of clover, the inner bark of the hemlock tree, and seaweed were all sometimes used as foods but none of these was very tasty.

Berries   Berries—strawberries, huckleberries, cranberries, soap berries—were everywhere, but they were hard to keep because they molded quickly in the wet climate. Some berries were stored in olachen or whale oil.

ALASKA

The first people of the far north lived mainly on meat.[7] They ate nearly every part of each animal they killed—including the contents of its stomach. (In a caribou's stomach, for example, there would be green plants, which were hard for the people to find otherwise.)

Even their "special treats" were high in nutrition; these were raw seal liver (vitamins A and C); *muktuk*, the raw skin of the white whale or narwhal (vitamin C); and partly digested shrimp from a whale's stomach, which they made into a rich paste that was full of minerals.

The early people of the Alaskan tundra cooked in their sunken houses over fires fueled by fatty animal bone or driftwood. They preferred caribou or musk ox meat, but also ate seal, polar bear, walrus, birds, and, when possible, trout and salmon.

An Aleut house was often filled with the smell of aging food. This didn't bother the Aleuts who preferred their fish and meat slightly decayed. Maybe such foods were easier to chew and digest as their fibers would be somewhat broken down by the aging process. Because wood was scarce, the Aleuts prepared their food over whale oil lamps or small fires of moss or bone that had been soaked in whale oil. Such heat sources would not thoroughly cook food, another reason, perhaps, for letting the meats age.

On their treks to and from the coast, when an actual fire couldn't be built, the Alaskan Eskimo wife set her flat soapstone lamp on a small portable table. With her musk-ox horn mallet, she pounded a piece of frozen whale blubber until it was soft and dripping. Then she laid the fat on the back half of her lamp. As it melted she put little chopped moss "wicks" along the edges of the fat and lighted the fire with embers she had brought along. Now the lamp gave off a smokeless flame over which she suspended a soapstone pot. In it a piece of caribou meat would soon give her family a rich broth for supper.

EsKimo Stone & Pottery Lamps

Starvation was always a threat during winter. In fact, many communities completely died out in years when sealing was bad and no other game was in sight.[8]

Meat

Caribou   This large North American relative of the reindeer was the main inland food source of the early people of Alaska. A fast, skilled hunter might kill 10 of these animals in a single hunt.

In the summer the huge caribou herds broke into smaller groups that grazed and fattened on the tundra. In September they formed large herds again and began heading south. This was the time for caribou hunts.[9]

Seal   The Inuits and Aleuts relied heavily on the seal for food.[10] There are two kinds of seal: the bearded (as big as seven feet long, and weighing 600 pounds) and the more common ringed seal (weighing 200 pounds).

In winter, when the ocean in northern Alaska froze to a depth of six or seven feet, the people hunted seals through the ice. (See **Tools and Gear,** hunting.)

On the killing of each seal, the animal was politely offered "a drink of fresh water" and then thankful prayers were given to its spirit for having allowed this animal to be taken for food.

Whales   If the whale hunt[11] was successful, the whale was towed to shore, a job that could take hours. There, its head was cut off and the wife of the successful harpooner poured fresh water into its blowhole, saying: "Here is water. You will want a drink. Come back next spring to our boat once more." She also asked the spirit of the whale to go to the Land of the Dead and report how respectfully it had been treated.

The whale was then butchered, the meat divided, and much of it buried in the semi-frozen ground. The whale's fat—the blubber—was made into oil, or stored to be traded to the inland people for furs and hides.

Walrus   The 2-ton Pacific Walrus traveled in herds, appearing each June on ice floes going north. Then the Inuit harpooned them from their open-decked boats, *umiaks*. Only the walrus flippers (which were left to ripen before being cooked) were eaten by these people. The rest of the walrus was stored and used throughout the winter as dog food.

WALRUS

The sea was shining brightly
near my hut.
I couldn't sleep.

I paddled out.
A walrus came
up by the boat.

He was too close for
a harpoon throw.
So I drove it
down and into him,
and the float went
hopping across the water.

But up he came,
and laid his flippers
just like elbows
on the surface,
as he tried to tear the float to bits.

He tired himself in vain:
an unborn lemming's skin
(my lucky charm)
was sewn to it.
Blowing angrily,
he gathered all his strength,
but I closed in
and put him out of pain.

—AUA IGLULIK, ESKIMO[12]

Polar Bears   The Inuit respected this huge animal, which could weigh as much as 1600 pounds, and also valued its meat for food.[13]

Wolves, Foxes, and Other Small Animals   These were caught in pitfalls and traps. An especially fiendish trap had spikes made of caribou bone set in the ice and covered with blood: a wolf would be drawn to the smell of the blood and would try to lick it off; in so doing, he would slash his own tongue, causing blood to flow. He would continue to lap the blood, now mostly his own, until he bled to death.

Fish   Between winter freeze and the annual move to the coastal seal camps was the time for an Inuit man to fish through the ice, which took hours of bone-chilling waiting.[14] If the summer hunts had been very good, he might not need to ice fish!

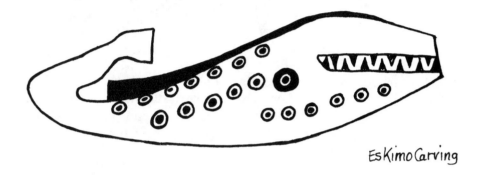

Eskimo Carving

Notes for "Food":

1. The early peoples gave thanks to the Great Spirit each time they gathered food. They never killed or took home more food than could be used by their family or tribe.

2. This sounds like a lot of nuts, but it wasn't: remember that each nut had to be cracked and the shell discarded. Only the kernel that remained was ground into meal. A family could use 500 to 800 pounds of acorn meal in one year!

3. *Here's how it was often done*: A hole was made in clean hard-packed sand along a stream. (In mountain areas the women lined each hole with pine needles.) The acorn meal was put into the hole. (Pine boughs were put on top.) Warm water was gently poured over the meal; this leached out the tannic acid into the surrounding sand. Once the water had gone through, the women skimmed off the processed meal and then dried it before cooking.

4. The Pomo, Maidu, Yuki, and Coast Miwok *did* hunt bear.

5. Baking and steaming were done outdoors in three-foot deep pits. A fire was made with rocks on top of it. Once the earth and rocks were hot, the ashes were removed and green herbs and leaves were spread on the stones. Then the meat and vegetables were put on and covered by another layer of leaves; hot coals and soil were added to refill the pit. In this way salmon berry shoots cooked in ten to fifteen minutes, a roast in three hours; but tough camas roots could require two to three days to bake!

6. *Life Cycle of the Pacific Salmon*:

   Between May and November most salmon battle their way upstream from the sea to spawn in the *same* freshwater stream in which they *hatched*; the females lay

thousands of eggs in redds (shallow gravel nests). Then the males fertilize the eggs and cover them with gravel. After spawning, both the males and females grow weak and die; bears and eagles feast on them. Their decomposing bodies give rich nutrients to the invertebrates in the stream bed, which in turn become food for next year's salmon!

The salmon eggs hatch in the winter or spring; at this stage they are called "alevins," and they stay in the gravel until each absorbs its yolk sac. They are called "fry" when they leave their gravel beds. Some species migrate at once to the sea, while others stay in freshwater up to 24 months before reaching the ocean, at which point they are called "smolts."

There are five types of Pacific salmon:

King (Chinook)—30 pounds, the world record being 97 pounds. They live 2 to 7 years.

Silver (Coho)—normally weigh 6 to 12 pounds and live 1-1/2 to 3-1/2 years.

Red (Sockeye)—6 to 12 pounds.

Chum (Dog)—weigh from 4 to 30 pounds and live 2 to 5 years.

Pink (Humpbacks)—2 to 4 pounds and live 2 years.

7. Giant kelp, cranberries, and sarana lily bulbs were dried during the summer and fall, and eaten throughout the winter. Usually the stored food supplies would run out just as the first birds returned in the spring.

8. Sometimes these early people survived only by cannibalism. A newborn baby girl might, in extreme circumstances, be strangled by her mother, allowed to freeze, and later used to feed the starving group.

9. *Hunting Caribou*: Once caribou was sighted, the hunter—staying downwind—hid himself until he could hit the animal with an arrow. If there was no place to hide, the man imitated the animal; he hunched over, used his bow and arrows as "antlers," and pretended he was grazing until he was close enough to strike.

Sometimes groups of hunters worked together: half as beaters, howling like wolves and driving the animals into a corral, and half as shooters, killing the trapped animals.

Using a corral
to hunt caribou.

When the caribou moved south, they had to cross lakes. The hunters waited until the animals were in the water and then jumped into their kayaks and speared the caribou in the backsides or kidneys. Any animals that turned toward shore were frightened back by screams from the women and children. If the herd was large, a man could kill ten animals in an afternoon.

10. The *Umealiq*, the leader of the winter camp, decided where and when to go seal hunting. One way was to go out in a kayak to where the seals were. These animals are, by nature, so curious that they would swim right up to the kayak to check it out. Then, when they sensed danger, they became motionless—perfect targets for the harpoon!

Ivory Cord Handle

Sometimes the men would hurl harpoons through ice holes or they would use underwater nets to snare the seals. Some hunters mimicked seals by slithering across the ice, or they hid behind blocks of ice that they slid forward until they were close enough to jump up and kill their prey!

At the end of March seals came up onto the ice to give birth; the baby seals were then easily clubbed.

11. *The Whale Hunt*: When whales were sighted, the *umiaks* were launched. The harpooner stood in the bow, six men rowed, and in the stern sat the crew leader—owner of the boat and gear—steering the boat with a paddle. He wore a raven skin amulet (good luck charm) and gave permission to the other men to sing whaling chants, which would call the whales and weaken them for the kill.

When a whale dived, the crew paddled as fast as they could, singing whale chants as loud as possible. The crew leader steered the umiak to where he expected the whale to come up out of the water. When it did, the man in the bow hurled the harpoon deep into the animal. The line attached to the harpoon whizzed overboard and whipped the sealskin drags (floats) into the sea. The whale dove down; each time it surfaced, another harpoon was thrust into its side. At last it would grow so weak that it would just lie on the surface of the water. Then the harpooner would raise a heavy, stone-pointed lance and, aiming for the heart or lungs, would *stab* the creature. A huge thrashing followed; the Inuit hunters, who were poor swimmers, had to be careful not to be thrown overboard. Once the whale spouted blood, the hunt was over.

12. From *Eskimo Poems from Canada and Greenland* by Tom Lowenstein, published by University of Pittsburgh Press, 1973, page 61.

13. *Hunting Bear*: The men and dogs followed a bear's tracks; when the bear was spotted, the dogs were unleashed. They "hounded" the bear and kept it at bay. If the men had a heavy spear on hand, they used it, while still keeping a safe distance, to wound the bear. Otherwise, they attacked the beast with their bow and arrows or their seal harpoons. It was extremely dangerous work and the fight could last for hours. Usually the bear was killed, eventually, and then the hunters shared the meat; the hide went to the man who was believed to have given the bear its final death thrust.

The hide was hung outside for five days, the length of time they believed the bear's spirit remained on the end of the weapon that had killed it. Each day they put small gifts on the bearskin, in the belief that it would help the bear's spirit to leave in peace.

14. A hole was chopped through the fresh ice in the river. A hookless lure (a strip of salmon bellyskin or a tiny carved ivory fish) was tied to the end of a short stick. The lure was put through the hole in the ice and twitched every few seconds by the fisherman. Once a fish was sighted, the lure was drawn up; if the fish followed, it was stabbed with a three-pronged spear.

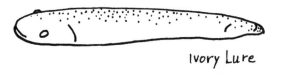

Ivory Lure

CLOTHING

CALIFORNIA

Because their weather was usually warm and sunny, early California people wore little or no clothing. The materials they used for their few clothes depended on the natural resources of the area in which they lived.

Many Indian women of central and southern California wore two-piece skirts of beaten fiber—cedar, cottonwood, redwood, willow, tule, or agave. Northern California women wore deerskin[1] skirts that were fringed and decorated with shells, seeds, and nuts.

Yurok   Maple bark skirt

When the weather was good, early California men either wore nothing or a deerskin breechcloth. A thin strip of leather went around the man's waist. A long piece of tanned deerskin went between his legs and up under the thin belt both in front and in back. The two ends of the deerskin hung down as an apron and a flap. The belt could also be used to hold a knife, a rabbit stick, or a flint.

Blankets and Capes

When the weather turned cold the early California natives wore capes or blankets made from rabbitskin ropes,[2] woven plants, deerskin (northern California), or bird feathers (Sacramento Valley).

Woven Basket Caps

Chumash and Cahuilla women wore these basket head coverings as a part of their every-day dress; among the Salinan and northern Maidu, *everyone* wore these woven caps. These head coverings were not only decorative, they also protected the woman's skin when she used the tumpline across her forehead to carry a heavy burden basket full of acorns or a load of firewood.

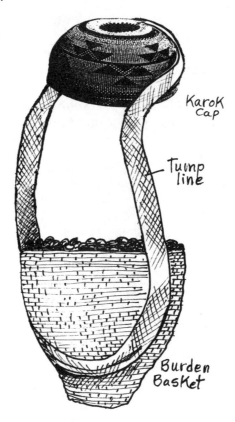

Karok Cap

Tump line

Burden Basket

Footwear

Usually these early people went barefoot unless it was very cold or they were going on a long trip. The Miwok, Maidu, and Pomo—among others in northern California—used ankle-high shoes made from one piece of buckskin with a seam up the heel and the front. Sometimes bearskin or elk hide soles were added, as among the Modoc.

The Pomo, who lived where tules grew, wove sandals out of the rushes. (See Photo 2.)

The California desert tribes wore deerskin boots that reached halfway up the calf as protection against thorns and snakes.

Those people who lived near swamps made big round tule frames for their feet that, when worn, kept them from sinking into the mud.

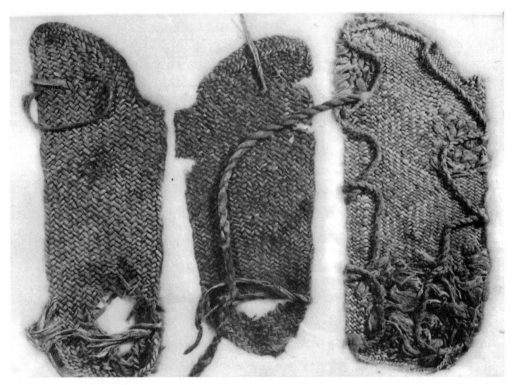

Photo 2. Pre-Columbian woven sandals made of yucca leaf, A.D. 1000-2000; circa 1940. *Photo by Wyatt Davis. Courtesy Museum of New Mexico.*

In the north snowshoes were made of willow, rosebud, or hazel wood formed into oval- or diamond-shaped frames that were faced with wild iris or grapevine netting. These snowshoes were tied on with deerskin thongs.

Decoration

Ornaments, often made of seashells or soapstone, were worn by both men and women.

Inuit Sea Mammal Tooth
NecKlace

Bone `needle` beads
California and the Northwest

Tattoos

Tattoos were worn by the women of some early California tribes.[3] They were usually applied to girls when they were between twelve and fifteen years old.

Tattoos were made by cutting the skin with an obsidian splinter or a flint blade, or with the needle from an agave or cactus. When blood came out of the cut, soot or charcoal dust was rubbed into the wound to make a black tattoo; grass dye or spider web was used to get a blue-green color. Being tattooed was painful and took a long time.

Yuki   Chimariko   Wailaki

California Facial Tattoos

Cosmetics

The Mojave, among others, painted their bodies and faces on an everyday basis; this protected their skins from insects, wind and weather, and helped keep the glare of the sun out of their eyes. They also felt that such painting made them more beautiful.

OREGON AND WASHINGTON

The inland people and those who lived at the heads of inlets in the far north wore tailored skin clothing.

The coastal people wore simple robes or cloaks woven of cedar bark yarn, mountain goat wool, and dog hair. On warm days the men wore nothing but their ornaments, while the women wore fringed aprons made of shredded cedar bark or rushes.

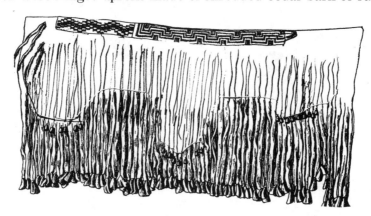

Footwear

The coastal people often went barefoot, as moccasins were unsuitable for the dampness, and sandals were unknown to them.

The inland people wore woven tule sandals in places where these rushes grew; elsewhere, they wore moccasins.

Robes

Shredded yellow cedar bark robes were worn for warmth. These had strips of very soft fur, such as otter, sewn along the upper edge for decoration.

Skin robes were rather stiff and had fur on one side; the women dressed the hides by rubbing animal brain on them.

Small pelts, such as sea otter, might be sewn together to make a robe prized for its warmth and softness.

Hats

Along the lower Columbia River and south of there, women wore small brimless basketry caps.

Wide-brimmed hats made of closely twined plant strands were worn from the Columbia River northward. Each hat was woven with an inside hat band so that it fit the head tightly. A chin strap was used on windy days.

Makah Woven Hat

Haida Rain hat

Rain Capes

These capes were water repellent rather than waterproof. They were made of thick strands of shredded red cedar bark or rushes and were slipped over the head, like a serape. The flared edge came just below the elbow, leaving the arms free. The neck band was often fur-lined to protect the neck from being rubbed by the bark.

Twisted Cedar Bark
Rain Cape

The Salish strung cattail stems together, using a long wooden needle, to make a raincoat.

Ornaments

Ornaments were worn by both men and women. The amount and kind of decoration they wore depended on their daily work and their place in the community.

Dentalium shells (see **Trade**) were used in necklaces or in clusters that hung from holes pierced in the person's ears or nasal septum.

Labrets

A labret is a decoration placed in a slit in the lower lip. Some Pacific Northwest women wore labrets made of wood or bone. The slit in the lip was enlarged over the years until an older woman was able to wear a three-inch labret!

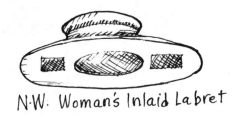

N.W. Woman's Inlaid Labret

Tattoos

In the Pacific Northwest tattoos were common, especially toward the north, where young highborn children were decorated with family crest designs.

Cosmetics

Decorative face and body painting, especially crest designs and symbols, were used for special occasions. In the northern parts of this region, early people used small stamps to make repeated patterns on the skin.

Everyday cosmetics were made by combining a grease (deer tallow) and pigments (red or yellow clay). They were applied to the face to prevent sun- and windburn.

ALASKA

Tlingit women wore white tanned caribou dresses. Tlingit men—as well as inland men and women, such as the Kutchin—wore pullover shirts and trousers of caribou leather. These were often decorated with porcupine quillwork or seeds or dentalium shells.

Mittens were worn by all Alaskan peoples. The Kutchins' mittens were on a cord that ran through the sleeves of the shirt to prevent their loss.

Eskimo clothing had to be protective and, at the same time, *flexible*, guarding the wearers against freezing winds and yet allowing them to move about easily. Alaskan Eskimo clothing was made mostly from seal or caribou skins[4]; also used were bird pelts, the hides of ground squirrels, marmots and hares, and even the intestines of some sea mammals!

Parkas

It took three caribou skins to make a parka; one for the front, one for the back, and one for the sleeves. Cut to loosely follow the body's outline, a parka was worn belted tightly to keep out drafts of cold air. It could be worn with its hood up for complete protection, or with the hood tossed back when it wasn't needed.

Northwestern Alaskan people wore long caribou parkas that reached to the knees and ended in rounded flaps trimmed with fur.

The looseness of the heavy folds allowed a layer of warm air to form next to the body.

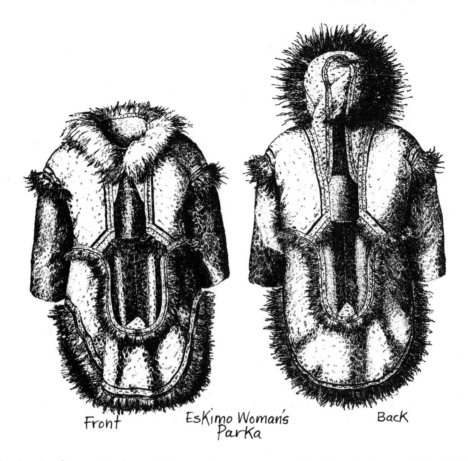

Front   EsKimo Woman's   Back
                  Parka

The back of a mother's sealskin parka was cut so that her baby could be held inside the jacket against her skin, where the little child would always be warm.

The Aleuts wore waterproof parkas, or long hooded overdresses, sewn from lengths of *ugruk* (OO-gruk), bearded seal intestine; these came down over the tops of their sealskin pants.

Footwear

The Aleuts wore ankle-high boots called *mukluks* and, also, leather boots that were high topped.

The inland people had moose-skin moccasins that were often attached directly to their trouser legs.

The Alaskan Eskimos wore socks and boots, with fur overshoes. Hunters in winter wore four layers of caribou fur on their feet.

The Inuit tied snowshoes and ice crampons to their shoes in order to keep them from sinking into snow or slipping on ice. The crampons worked like tire chains in snow.

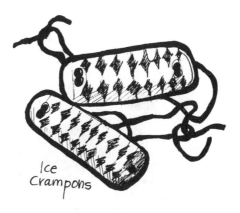

Ice Crampons

Hats

Haida and Tlingit women wove twined basketry hats; the men used crushed minerals mixed with fish roe to paint decorations on the hats. Some Tlingit hats were carved of wood and had rings on top to show the number of potlatches (see **Social Groups and Government**) the wearer had hosted.

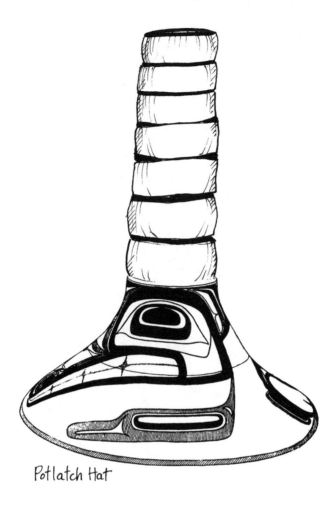

Potlatch Hat

The Aleuts and Yupiks wore hats with visors to cut down on the sun's glare off the sea.[5]

Sun Visor Hat

Body Ornaments

Labrets (lip plugs) were worn by some Tlingit women. Each was inserted into a slit in the skin. Often a Tlingit man wore a ring through his nose.

Some Inuit men wore bone or ivory labrets at each corner of the lower lip.

Eskimo
Lip Plugs,
Labrets

Tattoos of family crest figures were sometimes worn on the chests of Haida men.

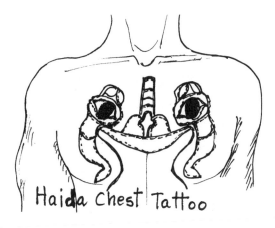

Haida Chest Tattoo

Notes for "Clothing":

1. *Hides for deerskin clothing were dressed (processed) in the following way*: The deer hide was buried in wet earth for several days (or soaked in water) to loosen its hairs. Next, the hair was removed with a scraper made from a deer rib or leg bone or from chert (a flinty rock). Then the hide was soaked in a mixture of deer brains and oak gall or ashes. Finally, the hide was pulled, stretched, and kneaded until it was soft and flexible. (The very softest hides were used for baby blankets.)

2. Every member of a family had his or her own robe, which provided protection even against freezing temperatures.

   Rabbit-skin blankets were used widely by the California groups, from as far south as the Tipai to as far north as the Washoe; this is how these robes were made:

   a. An obsidian knife was used to make a long continuous spiral cut on each rabbit skin; this made a rawhide strip 12 to 15 feet long.

   b. The strips made from three or four skins were tied together (making a strip about 40 feet long) which was then tied to a tree, dampened, twisted to form a rope, and left to dry.

   c. Four or five such rabbit-skin ropes were woven together (with milkweed fibers or Indian hemp) to form a very warm cape or blanket.

3. Among the Mojave, both men and women wore tattoos.

4. In late autumn the women prepared the winter wardrobes. For many days the wife sewed coats, pants, boots, and stockings for the family. When they were finished, she added white fur borders and decorative designs, sometimes even on inner surfaces which only the wearer would see!

5. Goggles and eye shades of carved wood or ivory were worn in the Arctic to protect against snow blindness. They cut down the glare that reflected off of snow and ice.

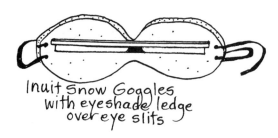

Inuit Snow Goggles
with eyeshade ledge
over eye slits

SHELTER

CALIFORNIA

California had the greatest variety of shelters of any region in North America, and some of the earliest known, as well.[1] How the shelters were built depended on the weather, what materials were available, and tribal tradition.

Sand-Roofed Houses

Mojave and Quechan   Yuman-speaking groups lived in *rancherías* (settlements) of two to three large houses. The center posts of these houses were eight feet tall and the side posts were four feet. The front wall was made of arrowweed packed between the upright posts. The roof of overlapping poles was covered with sand and was used for storage, resting, and visiting. A blanket or skins hung over the door opening to protect the inside from sand and heat. There was usually a ramada attached to the house to provide shade. (See Photo 3.)

Photo 3. Quechan sand-roofed house. *Courtesy American Museum of Natural History.*

Dome-Shaped Grass Houses

Photo 4. Woman with tules. *Courtesy Yakima Valley Regional Library, Relander Collection.*

Chumash and Gabrielino   Tall dome-shaped houses, common throughout much of southern California, were built on a frame of poles of debarked willow or sycamore "as thick as a man's arm." (See Photo 4.) The poles were cut 18 to 20 feet in length and were each set into the ground "a step apart" to form a circle 15 to 20 feet across; then the poles were lashed together at the top. One pole was left taller than the rest to prop open the smoke-hole cover. (See Photo 5.)

Next, horizontal stringers were lashed in tiers onto the frame; grass (brush or tule) was fastened in overlapping rows onto these tiers. The thick ends of the stems were left touching the ground and served to keep out stray animals. These rows of grass were then trimmed like bangs. (See Photo 6.) Sometimes side holes were cut for windows. The door was a huge tule mat; other tule mats were hung inside the building to form "rooms." Finally, the floor was sprinkled with water and then pounded to make it hard and smooth.

The Chumash even made a little "door bell" out of limpet shells strung together and hung outside the door.

Photo 5. Grass house under construction. *Courtesy Smithsonian Institution, National Anthropological Archives.*

Photo 6. Chumash grass house. *Photo by John P. Harrington. Courtesy Santa Barbara Museum of Natural History. (Originally Smithsonian Institution, National Anthropological Archives.)*

Thatched Grass and Brush Shelters

Costanoan, S. Cahuilla, S. Valley Yokut, Pomo, Wappo, and Others   These shelters were round or oblong and came in many sizes.[2] The floor was two feet below ground level and the frame was made from willow poles bent to make a rounded conical shape, something like a tall beehive. (See Photo 7.)

Photo 7. Pomo tule house. *Photo by C. H. Merriam. Courtesy Loure Museum of Anthropology, University of California at Berkeley.*

The frame was covered with brush or tule tied with cord made from hemp, nettle, or milkweed fiber. A smoke hole was left open at the top.

This Yokut shelter had a ridge pole supported by two posts, one at each end of the house. (See Photo 8.)

Photo 8. Yokut grass house. *Courtesy Bancroft Library, University of California at Berkeley.*

Large communal brush buildings housed several families. Each structure had an oblong floor; poles in two rows down the long side of the building held up the enlarged roof.

Many California villages had lean-tos, flat-topped brush shelters that provided shade during the hot summer months. Some tribes moved to the cooler hills during the summer and used these simple structures as temporary homes.

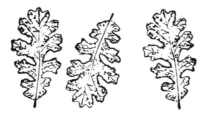

Houses with Earth Coverings

Luiseño, Central Miwok, Tipai, Ipai, Northern Yokut, North Central Yana and Yuki   In places where the weather was sometimes harsh, people built pole-framed brush houses with floors that were deeply dug out. Then they covered these shelters with earth; this combination helped the people keep cool in summer, and warm on cold nights and in winter. Inside an earth lodge, with a small fire going, it was quite warm.

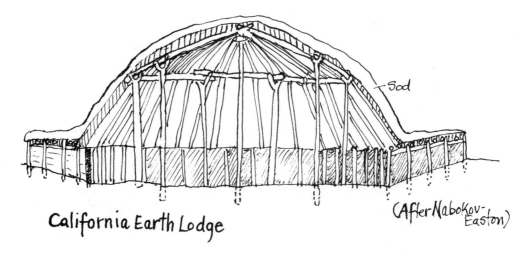

California Earth Lodge   (After Nabokov-Easton)

"Yet you have to be Indian to stand the crowding, the lack of privacy, the eternal squabbling of babies. . . . And after a few months of occupancy the vermin were terrible. Once in a while someone would take out the old litter and bring in a fresh supply of pine boughs. But the fleas, lice, cockroaches, and other bugs soon returned, and made life once more a misery. People sighed for the coming of spring, and quarreled as to what month they were in. The old chiefs were consulted, but they disagreed. . . . And so winter passed."

—Jaime de Angulo,
Jaime de Angulo Reader

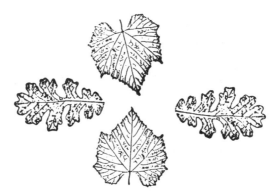

Bark Houses

Mono, Maidu, Nomlaki/Wintu, and Others   Mountain people used elk-horn wedges to split thick slabs of bark from redwood or cedar trees. (See Photo 9.) The bark slabs were leaned against a central pole to make a cone-shaped building. A smoke hole and an

Photo 9. Mono bark-covered house. *Photo by C. H. Merriam. Courtesy Loure Museum of Anthropology, University of California at Berkeley.*

entrance were left open in each house; this entrance was covered during winter by an animal skin or a tule mat.

These structures (8 to 15 feet in diameter) were big enough to sleep six or more people in winter; in summer, when people lived outdoors, these buildings became store-houses.

Plank Houses

Yurok (Redwood)[3], Hupa* (Cedar with Stone Foundations), Karok, Shasta and Tolowa
These family houses were found near the California-Oregon border and were similar in many ways to ones built further north. They were nearly square (an 18' x 20' floor was common) and partially underground; there was a central pit four to five feet deep. (See Photo 10.)

Photo 10. Yurok house with carved door plank. *Courtesy State of California Dept. of Parks & Recreation Photo Files.*

* United States publications, including U.S. geological maps and Bureau of Indian Affairs publications, use the spelling Hoopa when referring to the Hoopa Valley Reservation and its tribal members. The people themselves prefer the more traditional spelling Hupa to be used when referring to the tribe and its members.

A plank house of redwood or cedar slabs[4] was built over the sunken floor. From outside the walls and roof of this plank house looked low, but once inside you could easily stand up. (See Photo 11.)

Photo 11. Hupa 3-pitch family house of split cedar planks with low wall of river rocks. *Courtesy San Diego Museum of Man.*

Outside, horizontal willow or hazel poles were lashed in place with tough vines to give support to the slab wall.

These solid houses were warm in winter and cool in summer.

The Hupa plank house had a clean flat floor with a square sunken living-room area that was reached by a ladder. The walls of this sunken room were lined with planks. A fire was built in the middle and here the family cooked and ate. A few feet back from the pit, thick wallboards were stood upright in the ground to form a storage shelf. Here baskets of dried foods, firewood, and tools were kept, as well as mats for sitting and sleep-

The interior of Plank House

ing. Men and special visitors sat (or slept) farthest from the door and its possible drafts; next came the women and children, while the least important sat or lay right next to the door.

Ceremonial Round Houses

Most California tribes had these community buildings and used them for dances and religious ceremonies.

The Pomo dug a hole 5 feet deep and 50 feet wide, setting aside the dirt they collected to later be used on the roof. Five big posts, 18 feet tall, held up the roof beams, which were covered with brush over which the collected dirt was packed. Such a round house could hold as many as 700 people!

Pomo Communal House Plan
(After Nabokov)

Sweat Houses

Here men cleansed themselves, smoked, held council, and got ready for social and religious affairs. (See Photo 12.)

Photo 12. Luiseño sweat house, 1885. *Courtesy California Historical Society, Los Angeles, collection of historical photographs, #4960. Malcolm Margolin loan.*

In southern California, sweat houses were cone-shaped and mud-plastered. The Chumash had the largest, which were up to 12 feet in diameter. They entered such a sweat house by a side door, or down a pole ladder through the smoke hole.

Most California sweat houses used the dry heat of an almost smokeless fire that was fed by willow twigs.

In northern California the sweat house had a floor of polished wood or earth. There could even be stone retaining walls and a sunporch. (See Photo 13.)

Photo 13. Yurok sweat house interior. *Photo by Peter Nabokov.*

From outside this building looked as if the roof had collapsed on the ground. (See Photo 14.)

Photo 14. Karok sweat house, Klamath River. *Courtesy Siskiyou County Museum.*

The men entered through a small door in the roof and left by a hole in a subterranean trench. Whenever a sweat house was built or rebuilt, it was done with the greatest respect. As the Yurok said, "This is the purest of buildings."

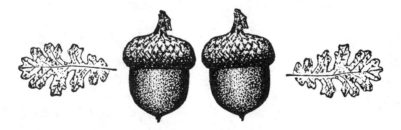

OREGON AND WASHINGTON

Coastal Plank Houses

Tillamook, Chinook, Quinault, Coastal Salish and Makah   These coastal people lived in their winter plank houses from October to May. (See Photo 15.) These buildings varied a bit from place to place (as to length, number of ridge poles, type of roof)[5]; but, on the whole, Pacific Northwest plank shelters shared these features:

- They were built on a beach facing out onto the water.
- The houses were usually rectangular in shape.
- Logs were used for the posts outlining the building.
- Huge logs were used for the beams that spanned the width of each building.
- Long ridge poles ran front to back.
- Split cedar planks were used for the walls and the roof.
- No nails were used in the construction. The wall planks fit together tightly and perfectly because the joints were mortised. (A mortise is a notch or groove cut in one piece of wood to receive a projecting part of the piece to which it is joined.)
- The walls were nonsupporting and separate from the roof.[6]
- Sunken fire pit(s) heated the building.

Photo 15. Chinook house. *Reproduced from the collections of The Library of Congress, Washington, D.C.*

- There were no windows. Air came through a smoke hole in the roof that could be covered, in bad weather, by a sliding wooden panel.
- The front door was cut above the expected snow levels.

This carved Killer whale fin was probably used in a whaling ritual.

Ozette, a Makah village on the western tip of the Olympic Peninsula, was covered by a mudslide 450 years ago. Six shed-roofed houses and all their contents have been preserved in this "Native American Pompeii"—under 8 feet of mud. The houses held thousands of artifacts including baskets, toys, whaling gear, and a carved killer whale fin inlaid with over 700 sea otter teeth.

Plateau Shelters

Pit Houses   At first the peoples of the Plateau region of Oregon and Washington lived in pit shelters, North America's oldest type of house. (See Photo 16.)

Photo 16. The pit house, oldest type of North American house. *Courtesy American Museum of Natural History.*

Mat Houses   Over time mat shelters took the place of the pit houses. The common winter mat house was 25 to 60 feet long, 12 to 15 feet wide, and 10 to 14 feet high. Each mat house was formed over an **A-frame** structure of peeled poles. (See Photo 17.)

Photo 17. Frame of a mat house. *Courtesy Smithsonian Institution.*

The mat lodges that housed several families were up to 150 feet long and were built around a line of A-frames. (See Photo 18.)

Photo 18. Putting tule mats on house frame. *Photo by Dick Relander, 1952. Courtesy Smithsonian Institution, National Anthropological Archives.*

Summer Houses   During berrying and fishing seasons, Plateau people put up simple pole and mat shelters. (See Photo 19.)

Photo 19. Umitilla gable-roofed mat-covered house, 1950. *Courtesy Field Museum of Natural History.*

ALASKA

The Haida and Tlingit Indians lived in plank houses much like those of the Pacific Northwest. (See Photo 20.) Both Haida and Tlingit winter houses had these features in common:

- A square floor plan, about 40 feet long on each side.
- Mortised (tightly fitted) plank walls.
- Two roof beams and a gabled roof.
- A raised platform that ran around the inner walls.[7]
- Two floor levels; the second, lower level was two feet down and lined with cedar planks.

Photo 20. Haida Chief Gold's Moon House, 1895-1900. *Courtesy American Museum of Natural History.*

- Carved interior posts.
- A carved or painted rear screen that was set up for winter ceremonies.
- A central sunken fire pit with an adjustable smoke hole in the roof.
- Unpainted outer walls, as a rule.
- A door hole cut high enough to be above snow levels.
- Crest column(s) in front of the house.

The Haida Winter House

In the 18th century there were some 34 Haida villages spread along the Pacific coastline. (See Photo 21.) Early Haida houses used two central posts for support. With time, the Haida built six beam houses that did not need the central posts and this opened up the inside of each big house. An extraordinary example is the Monster House.[8]

Photo 21. Haida house frame, 1901. *Photo by C. F. Newcombe. Courtesy British Columbia Provincial Museum, Victoria.*

Haida houses had carved door posts as well as carved frontal and rear posts. (See Photos 22 and 23.)

Photo 22. Beam ends of Haida Eagle House. *Photo by Division of Photography. Courtesy Field Museum of Natural History.*

Photo 23. Rear post of Haida Raven House, Skidegate. *Courtesy Field Museum of Natural History.*

These carved posts showed short stylized family histories of the clans of both the husband and wife of the house. (See Photo 24.)

The Tlingit Winter Plank House

Long ago the Tlingit Nation had 40 winter towns spread along the Alaskan panhandle and islands. Some towns were made up of just a few houses, while others could have as many as 60 plank buildings, separated by clan into two rows, facing the coast. The houses stood right next to each other on the upper beach, usually behind a screen of crest columns (totem poles). (For "crests" and "clans," see **Social Groups and Government**.)

The Aleut Barabara

The Aleut barabara was one of the largest native homes in the North.[9] It was built half underground. Posts set six to seven feet inside the support walls held up the driftwood and whale-bone roof that was covered with thatch and sealed with grassy sod. The posts outlined the sleeping places, which were mat-draped trenches along the walls. Dried grass covered the floors. (See Photo 25.)

Photo 24. Frame of Haida two-beam house. *Courtesy Field Museum of Natural History.*

Photo 25. Inside an Aleut barabara, 1778. *Photo by J. Webber. Courtesy Smithsonian Institution.*

People entered a barabara by climbing down a notched log ladder that led through a hole in the roof into the main room. Tiny secret rooms were carved in the walls to be used as hiding places for the children during enemy attacks.

With time, each of these houses would become completely overgrown with grass, so that an Aleut village looked like a group of soft green mounds.

Pole House

On King Island at the entrance to the Bering Sea was Ukivik, an Eskimo village. The people there lived in stilt-supported houses: plank-framed boxes wrapped in walrus hide and tied with rope. The two-room buildings were held up by 20-foot high tree trunks; the people stored their hide boats in racks under the floors of the houses. Steep wooden staircases and plank ramps were the streets of this tiny town. (See Photo 26.)

Photo 26. Stilt-supported houses, King Island, 1928. *Photo by J. Webber. Courtesy Smithsonian Institution.*

Alaskan Eskimo Winter Houses

Although the igloo[10] comes to mind as "the typical Eskimo house," this snow-block structure was mainly used by the Central Arctic Eskimos of Canada. Much more common in northern Alaska were the permanent sod-roofed winter houses that were partly sunken into the ground and framed with stone, whale bone, or driftwood (depending on what materials were available), and covered over with dirt and sod. Where there was wood, logs were used to form the entryways and walls. (See Photo 27.)

The number and length of entry tunnels into a winter house varied, as did the location of sleeping platforms. The house was heated by a central fire or oil lamp(s).

In southernmost Alaska, some Eskimo groups used sod-covered gabled structures modeled after Northwest Coast plank houses.

Photo 27. Sod-roofed winter houses. *Photo by E. S. Curtis. Courtesy Santa Barbara Museum of Natural History.*

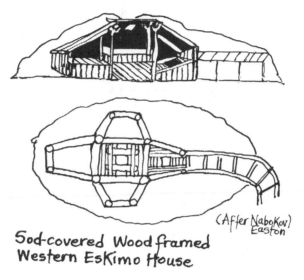

(After Nabokov)
Easton

Sod-covered Wood framed
Western Eskimo House

Tent

In May when the sod houses became soggy, Eskimos moved into some kind of tent (*tupik*). (See Photo 28.) The Alaskan Inuit made temporary shelters from the walrus-hide boats (*umiaks*) turned on their sides.

Photo 28. Alaskan Eskimo summer shelter made of walrus-hide boat (umiak) turned on its side. *Courtesy University of Washington.*

Kashim

Most Eskimo winter villages had an oversize building, a *kashim*, that was both a cere-monial center and a clubhouse for men. Here they gathered to socialize, gamble, and take sweat baths.

The kashim was the place for religious ceremonies, the curing of illnesses, and the initiation of the young. Some kashims had secret passageways *and* hidden trapezes that were used by shamans (*angakok*) for dramatic effects.

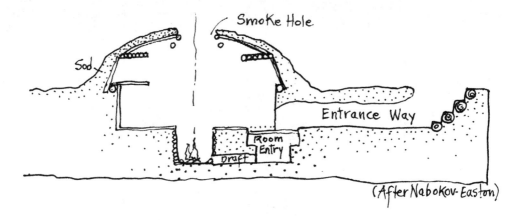

(After Nabokov-Easton)

The following Eskimo pictograph shows a curing ceremony in a kashim, while the villagers watch from the benches along the wall. Read from the top above the **T** pole: the shaman holds two lamps and chants to his seated patient (three drummers are behind him); (to the right) he drives out the bad spirit; (to the left) he chases the spirit toward the door with his curing charm while his two assistants (at the bottom) rush the evil spir-it out of the kashim for good!

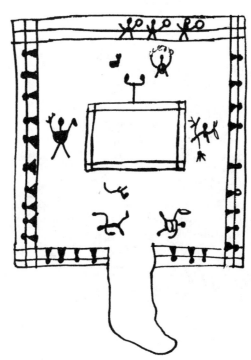

Notes for "Shelter":

1. The oldest North American Indian house has been found in eastern California near the Stanislas River. About 12 feet long and oval in shape, it was built 9,500 years ago!

2. The Yokuts, for example, built *five* different kinds of brush houses, including a large communal shelter that was practically a small village and could house five to six families. It was 300 feet long, roofed with tule matting, and had a main door at either end. Inside were private living areas, each with its own fire pit and its own separate entrance.

3. To the Yurok each redwood plank was a spirit and together the plank walls breathed and lived, just as the people did. Each house had a name, which also identified the family that lived there.

4. Slabs were gotten from fallen redwood or cedar trees or by burning a tree to make it fall. Deer or elk antler wedges were used to split tree trunks into planks that were not sanded, so that rain ran off the wood down its natural grooves. (To measure, men used the width of their fingers, breadth of hands, and distance between wrist/elbow and elbow/shoulder.)

5. Here are some specifics:

Chinook	14 to 20 feet wide and 20 to 60 feet long; single ridge pole; gable roofed; partly sunk living area
Tillamook	shed-roofed; plank-lined floor pit; small rectangular door in front wall
Quinault	gable-roofed; single ridge pole; oval door in front wall; plank porch with a bench in front of house
Coastal Salish	25 to 50 feet long; shed roofed; plain facade with door tucked in one corner and second door out back; roof planks and wall planks were bound with cedar bark ties to support poles; could hold 600+ people
Makah	30 feet wide by 70 feet long; shed-roofed; light let in and smoke released by moving roof boards (See Photo 29.)

6. Many Northwest Coast Indians took down the cedar plank sidings of their permanent winter houses and used them to build temporary summer shelters at their inland fishing camps. (See Photo 30.)

   The frame of the winter house would be left open until fall when the people came back and replaced the plank walls.

7. Along the back side of the platform were the families' sleeping areas; these were placed according to rank. The highest honor went to the chief's family, whose sleeping area was at the upper wall on the right, across from the doorway.

   The chief's family living area was set apart from the rest by a highly decorated screen. Two carved posts, one at each edge of this area, told the history of the chief's moiety. The high ranking families had wooden panels about their areas; the lower rank areas had simple mat "walls." (See Photo 31.)

Photo 29. Makah plank house. *Photo by E. S. Curtis. Courtesy Santa Barbara Museum of Natural History.*

Photo 30. Northwest fishing shelter. *Photo by F. Dally, 1867-1870. Courtesy British Columbia Provincial Museum, Victoria.*

Photo 31. Northwest coast lodge and Indians in front of Chief's house, Masset. *Courtesy American Museum of Natural History.*

8. The "Neuwons" or Monster House is the largest known Haida house. It was built around 1850 in the village of Masset. A chief Weah had it made to honor the marriage of his son to the daughter of a wealthy neighboring chief.

   The planks came only from standing trees; the cedar beams were brought from far off, dragged for many miles behind canoes. Two thousand workers built this house; it covered at least 55 square feet and had eight beams instead of the usual six. Inside were three floor levels with a central fireplace. This pit was lined with wide horizontal cedar planks.

   The original Monster House in time fell to pieces, but today we know its size because of a photograph that shows items such as the captain's chair whose exact dimensions are known; from these dimensions we can calculate the size of the house itself. (See Photo 32.)

9. A barabara that housed several families would be 40 to 65 feet long and 20 to 35 feet wide. Some were built 200 feet long, 40 feet wide, and housed 150 people!

10. At first, the Eskimo word *iglu* meant "any permanent roofed shelter made of solid materials: any winter house"; it was the non-Eskimos who used it to mean "a domed snow block shelter." Actually, most Eskimos used snow block igloos *only* for temporary protection: during a storm or while on a long trip.

Photo 32. Interior of Haida Monster House. *Courtesy University of Washington.*

TOOLS AND GEAR

We create tools to make our lives easier. Tools stab, cut, hold, scrape, and refine. The early Coastal people made tools that were artful in form and design, which brought the people pleasure *as* the tools were being used.

MATERIALS

The early California people had a great variety of materials from which to make tools. Plant fibers became extraordinary baskets, tule boats, and various traps. Steatite was carved into bowls, pestles, and ornaments. Asphaltum, a tar that oozed up from the beaches along the coastline, was used to waterproof boxes, boats, and baskets. Seashells were turned into tool blades, jewelry, utensils, and even doorbells! (See **Shelter**.)

Many of the same materials were available in the Pacific Northwest; but the people in Washington and Oregon had another great resource: cedar wood. They used it to make tools and then used these tools to create—from wood—buildings, seaworthy canoes, dishes, cradles, chamber pots, as well as ceremonial masks and totem poles.

Each carved item was beautifully designed and perfectly made—whether it was a box, a bowl, a rafter, or a rattle!

The coastal Arctic peoples had few materials from which to make tools: bone, hide, ivory, sinew, rock, and, once in a great while, wood. Their bows, harpoons, and sleds all had to be pieced together from whatever materials were at hand. A bow, for example, was backed with sealskin and braided sinew to keep it flexible; if there was no wood to use for sled runners, frozen leather was used. If there wasn't any leather? Frozen fish with antler crosspieces were lashed together to become sled runners! These northern people have always been ingenious.

HUNTING

Clubs, Bolas, and Atl-atls

A thrown rock was probably the very first hunting tool. Bolas were made from two or more stone weights tied together; the Eskimos used bone or ivory weights with either a feather or a straw rudder. Bolas were flung into the air to snare birds in flight. Clubs were used to kill trapped fish and game.

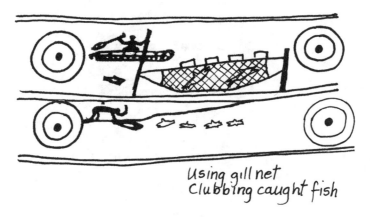

Using gill net
Clubbing caught fish

Atl-atls, hand-held spear throwers, were carved of wood or ivory.

Eskimo Atlatl

Bows and Arrows

The bow was made from yew or cedar and was polished with deer bone marrow to keep it flexible.

Modoc Painted Bow

Many California Indians used two-piece arrow shafts. The main shaft was often a piece of hollow cane. The point was attached to the end of the foreshaft, a short piece of solid wood that fit inside the main shaft.[1]

Flint Bear Arrowpoints, Bering Eskimo

Projectile Points and Knives

These were made from a hard stone like chert, obsidian, or jasper; in the north, ivory or bone was used. The point was attached to the arrow shaft and the shape of the point depended on the animal being hunted.

Other Hunting Gear[2]

The early people knew the habits and seasons for each kind of bird. The Coast Salish of Washington set up nets along the migratory paths of ducks, geese, and plovers. A pair of 40-foot high poles were raised and between them the men strung nets so fine that they were nearly invisible. At twilight the unsuspecting birds flew straight into these nets. The hunters gathered up the birds and wrung their necks.

Every hunting method known in early North America was used by the people of the Pacific Northwest, including stalking and group drives, with or without dogs. Bows and arrows, atl-atls, snares, nets, traps, pitfalls, and deadfalls were all used.

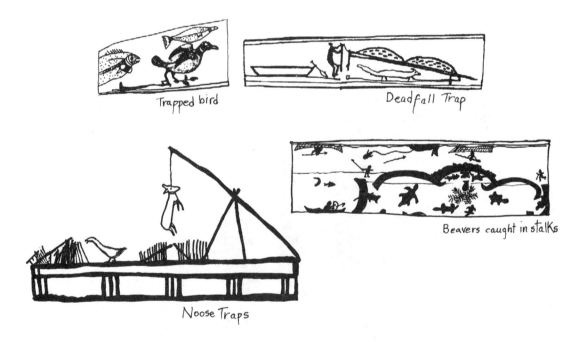

Trapped bird

Deadfall Trap

Beavers caught in stalks

Noose Traps

The coastal Arctic people needed special tools to deal with their cold climate.

Snow testers were used whenever the hunter was crossing land where icy pools of water might be hidden beneath the snow. To get wet feet in the Arctic *could* mean death!

The *seal scratcher* was made of real seal claws, attached to a handle. The Inuit used it to scratch on the surface of the ice so the seal under it would think there was "company" up on top and would come up to visit!

Inuits (wearing Intestine Parkas) using snow testers

Ivory Ice Scratcher

FISHING

Fishing was a matter of preparation, tools, knowledge, and luck. An early California fisherman hung fishing charms on a nearby tree or around his neck to bring the fish to his spot on the water!

Fishing Gear

Fishline, lures, fish hooks, spears, nets, and net weights were used throughout the coastal states.

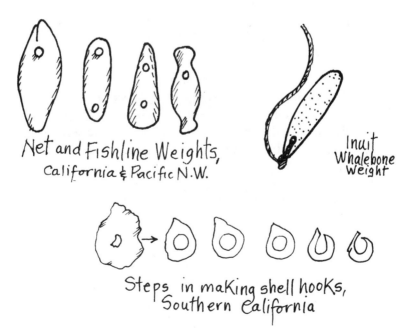

Net and Fishline Weights, California & Pacific N.W.

Inuit Whalebone Weight

Steps in making shell hooks, Southern California

Gorge hooks used by California fishermen caught in the stomach, or gorge, of the fish and kept the fish from escaping. Asphaltum "glued" the line to the center of the hook.

Bi-pointed
Gorge Hooks,
California

Pacific Northwest fishermen used halibut-style hooks. The halibut put its upper lip over the barb that held the bait; the line was attached to a hole in the upper part of this hook.

Halibut Hook,
Haida-Tlingit

The Inuit craftsman took such care with his creations that even his ivory fish hooks and lures were artful.

Ivory lures

The early people of central California would sometimes make a little hut or blind over a stream and spear fish as they swam past. The California spear was a long pole with an attached dagger that could be taken off and used as a knife.

The Inuit fish spear had three barbed bone tines: the middle point speared the fish and the two flanking barbs held on to it.

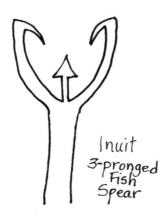

Inuit
3-pronged
Fish
Spear

Upstream
(Song of an old man salmon-fishing from the ice)

*I often go back
to my little song,
and hum it patiently
at my fishing hole on the ice.
Again and again,
I hum that simple little song.
I, who all too soon
get weary when I fish,
watchfully angling,
trying to tempt
the blue-back salmon with their glossy scales,
who swim,
          upstream.*

*Blowingly cold, my vigil on the ice.
I soon give up.
When I get home with insufficient catch
I say that it was the fish that failed,
          upstream.*

—from *Eskimo Poems of Canada and Greenland*

Weirs and Dipnets

Fishing was the main source of meat for the people of the Northwest. They used several different tools to make their catches.

Woven pole fences, called weirs, let water flow through while keeping back the fish, which could then be speared or netted. The huge long-handled nets used to scoop up the fish are known as dipnets.

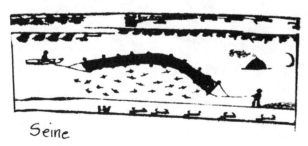

Seine

Dipnet

SEA HUNTING

Harpoons

Harpoons were spears fitted with barbs; they were used by the coastal peoples to hunt sea animals.

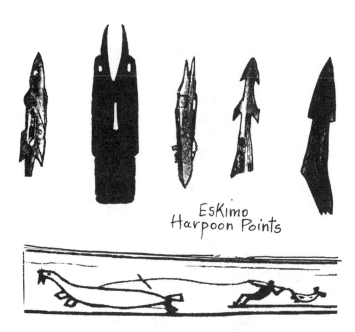

Eskimo
Harpoon Points

The deadly whaling harpoon used by Northwest coast and Alaskan sea hunters was an 18-foot long spear of heavy seasoned yew. It had a razor-sharp mussel shell blade backed by sharp bone spurs. Big sealskin floats[3] that slowed down the whale—and also kept its carcass above water—were firmly tied to the harpoon with sinew lines. The harpoon line could be used to tow the dead whale back to the shore.[4]

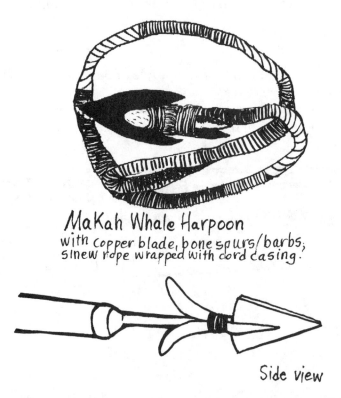

Makah Whale Harpoon
with copper blade, bone spurs/barbs,
sinew rope wrapped with cord casing.

Side view

An Inuit hunter carved a wolf on his harpoon, because this animal was known for its ability to track and kill its prey.

Boats

All of the early people along the Pacific used boats to get fish and game, as well as for transportation. Although made out of different materials, these vessels were all moved by the use of paddles.

Tule[5] Boat of California   The tule boat, made of tule reeds tied into a shape (with tough vines or twisted reed), was high in the front and back, and low on the sides; it could hold one or more people depending on its size.

Although these boats got water-logged after a few hours, they would quickly dry out in the hot sun. A tule boat lasted about a year.

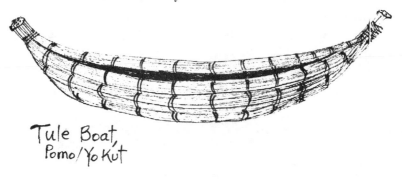

Tule Boat,
Pomo/Yo Kút

Sewed-plank Boat of Southern California   Sewed-plank boats were used to make long trips up and down the California coast and between the offshore islands. This boat is still a bit of a puzzle because no *complete* sewed-plank boat has ever been found. We do know that it was a canoe made of planks sewn together. Asphaltum, found on the beaches, was used to waterproof the cords and the holes in the wood.

Dugout Boats   The Yurok and the Hupa made dugout boats that were used mainly on rivers, like the Klamath, but not in deep water.

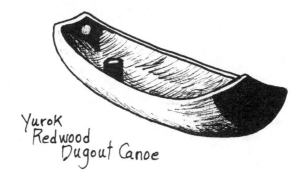

Yurok
Redwood
Dugout Canoe

Seagoing craft were built further up the Pacific Coast. Each of these dugouts was cut from a single red cedar or redwood log. Here are the steps involved in making such a boat:

1. The tree was felled,[6] its bark removed, the log split lengthwise, and turned round side up. An axe with a curved blade (an adze) and wedges were used to shape the bottom which was made two fingers thick. The sides were smoothed.

2. Mauls and wedges were used to clear out the inside part of the log. This took a long time and was hard work. The sides were made two fingers wide at the bottom and one finger wide at the top.

3. Now the inside of the boat was filled with water. Several fires were built close around the dugout to heat the outside of the boat. Very hot rocks were put inside the boat to make the water boil. Slowly the wood softened, and thwarts[7] were forced in to make the craft wider.

4. The stern and bow were carved. The stern piece was anchored in place with cedar pegs so tightly fitted that the seal was watertight.

5. Very long cedar strips were put on the sides of the boat to become the gunwales, which kept out the water. The hull was sanded and finished. (See Photo 33.)

The hull was elaborately decorated with carvings, paintings, and/or inlays of abalone shell.

The dugouts were carved and shaped to glide quickly and noiselessly through the water. Even though the canoe maker had no square, level, compass or blueprints, he built the boat beautifully.

Photo 33. Haida canoes. *Courtesy University of Washington.*

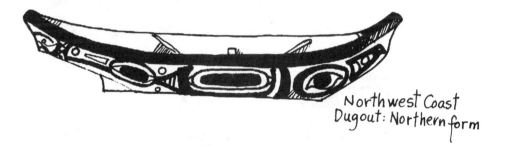

North west Coast
Dugout: Northern form

Kayak   The Alaskan kayak had a strong light frame and a watertight cover in which an opening was left for the paddler. The man's parka was lashed to this opening to make boat and man into a single waterproof unit.

Baidarka   The Aleutians built a kayak-like boat called a baidarka. It had a forked prow and handled well in rough seas. In a sudden storm the men strapped all the baidarkas together to create a large, and so a more stable, craft!

Baidarka

Umiak   The umiak was a large (up to 30 feet long) skin-covered boat with a sturdy frame. Sometimes fit with sails, it handled loads of more than a ton. It could carry families with *all* their possessions when people were moving between summer camps; at these times the women rowed with short quick strokes and a man in the stern guided the boat with a steering oar.

Harpooning whales   Umiaks with and without sails

Umiaks with sails

FOOD GATHERING

Digging Sticks, Root Adzes, and Seed Beaters

Special sticks were used by women for loosening the soil and digging up roots and bulbs. In southern California they were made of hard wood like mahogany. The Chumash even made them out of whale bone. In the Northwest digging sticks were made from tough spruce; those used for prying shellfish off rocks were carved to points on both ends.

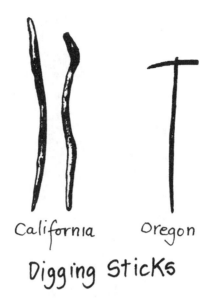

California   Oregon

Digging Sticks

Adzes with flint, bone, or ivory blades were also used to dig up roots.

Stone Adz
with leather knuckleguard

The Pomo, among others, used seed beaters to shake seeds off trees and bushes.

California
Seedbeaters
and Sifters

Burden Basket, Tumpline, and Small Bags

The California or Northwest Coast woman supported the burden basket (filled with wood or acorns) by a head strap (a tumpline) worn across her forehead and running back around, or under, the heavy basket itself. In California the tumpline might be made of wild iris leaves, nettle, hemp, or milkweed fiber. In the Northwest it was made of braided grass and the basket of beaten cedar bark.

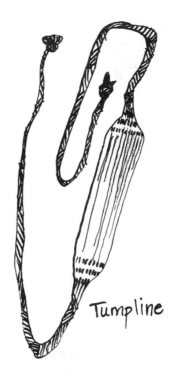

Tumpline

The net bag was used in a similar way to carry loads. In southern California the ends were tied to a cord or woven into a headband.

The northern Alaskan and Aleut people used bags and baskets made of woven grass.

Yurok - Hoopa Net Bag

FOOD UTENSILS

Grinders

Mortars and pestles in California were made of soapstone, lava rock, or stone boulders. To the north they were made of carved wood or large stones. (See Photo 34.)

Photo 34. Mojave people with mortar, pestle, and pots, 1883. *Photo by Ben Wittick. Courtesy Museum of New Mexico.*

Woman's Knife

Called a *ulu*, this knife was made with a slate blade.

Ulu with slate blade

Cooking Baskets and Tongs

Cooking baskets, used from southern California to northern Alaska, were woven to be hard and watertight. When half-filled with a liquid, they would not burn; but if the cook let the water boil away, the baskets could burn on the bottom—as we can see from the scorch marks on some of the ancient baskets found preserved at Ozette, Washington.

Looped tongs were used to drop clean heated stones into a basket of liquid. The tongs were later used to remove the cooled stones and replace them with newly heated ones. Wooden stirrers were used to mix the cooking soup or cereal.

California Cooking Basket

Cookware

Before pottery was made, carved stone "pots" were used for cooking.

Steatite was used to make dishes in which food was melted or cooked. In California each dish had a hole in its side so that it could be pulled off the fire with a hooked stick.

Northwest Cedar Cooking Boxes   These containers, which were used daily, were so well made that they were watertight; soups were cooked in them by the hot-rock method. These boxes were also used to carry water and store olachen or whale oil. (See **Arts and Crafts**.)

Cedar Box

Alaskan Cooking Buckets and Stone Stoves   In Alaska—in areas where wood *was* available—soups and broths were cooked by dropping hot rocks into a wooden bucket, made as shown in the following illustration.

Because many Inuits had little or no wood, they used stone stoves that burned oil with moss wicks.

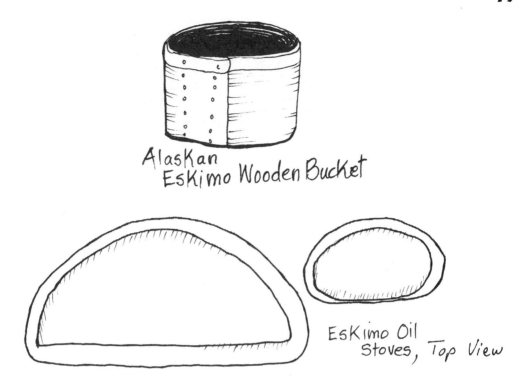

Alaskan
Eskimo Wooden Bucket

Eskimo Oil
Stoves, *Top View*

Serving Dishes and Spoons

Dishes woven of reed or made of abalone were used in California. Simple wooden bowls were used for daily eating in the Northwest and in Alaska.

In the Pacific Northwest, trough-like dishes—six feet or more in length—were used on feast days to serve up to a dozen people at one time. Alder was used to make these trenchers because it would not give the food an odd taste. Such dishes were highly decorated with carvings of both animals and people.

In California spoons were formed from shells or carved out of stone. The Northwest and Alaskan peoples used wooden spoons decorated with carved figures or painted designs. Inuits also used horn or ivory spoons.

WOODWORKING

The early people of the Northwest were woodcutters and expert woodworkers, using a wide variety of tools.

Knives, chisels, picks, drills, and adzes were made with blades of jadeite, shell, horn, beaver teeth, or bone.[8]

The craftsmen used wedges (made of yew wood or antler bones) that they hammered with stone mauls to split cedar into boards.

Antler Wedge

The surface of a fine wooden object was sanded with dogfish skin or scouring rushes to make it satin smooth.

MISCELLANEOUS TOOLS

Sewing tools were similar throughout the different regions, with local variations, of course.

Inuit Sewing Set

The basic Inuit sewing set included—in a sewing case—strands of sinew thread, ivory needle(s), an awl for making holes, a leather thimble (fingerstall), and a piece of jade for sharpening the awls and needles.

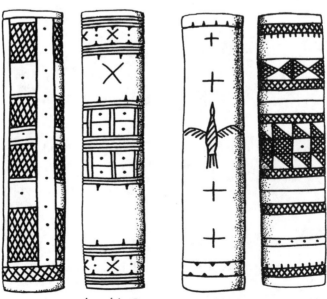

Inuit Carved Needle Cases

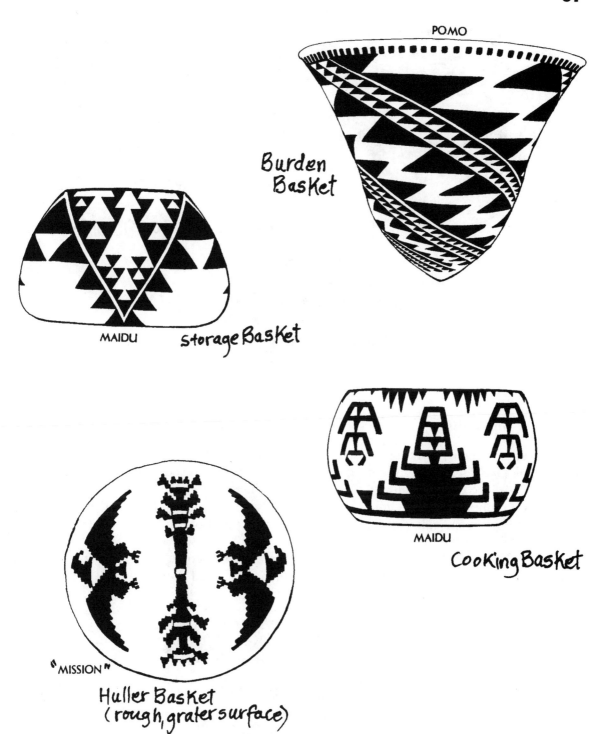

POMO

Burden Basket

MAIDU   Storage Basket

MAIDU   Cooking Basket

"MISSION"
Huller Basket
(rough, grater surface)

Special Baskets

In California the women wove and braided a huge variety of exceptionally beautiful baskets that were used as: sifters, parchers, hullers, winnowers, and storage containers. The grease strainer was a very unusual food preparation tool!

Jar Basket

California Baskets

Bowl Basket

Fire-Starting Tools

Fires were started by striking two stones (containing quartz, flint, or iron pyrite) together to make sparks that set tinder aflame. Or fire drills were used in the following way:

A flat piece of wood with shallow holes (the hearth) was laid on the ground. Dried leaves were put around the hole. A pointed hardwood stick (the fire drill) was steadily twirled, between the palms, in one of the holes. The point of the fire drill got hotter and hotter until it set the dry leaves on fire!

The Alaskan Eskimos sometimes used a team of two people to twirl and press down on the drill; this made a dust so fine that it would ignite when they blew on it. Dried moss was put in with the dust to keep the flame going.

Eskimo Fire-making Sets

Notes for "Tools and Gear":

1. A foreshaft arrow was easy and efficient to use. Once it entered the prey, only the main shaft had to be taken out of the animal. Another foreshaft was quickly fitted into the main shaft and the hunter was ready to shoot again!

2. Not all hunting tools were weapons. The Yokuts made a carrying cage for a decoy pigeon that they tied to a shelf on which bait was scattered; a blind was built behind this shelf. Wild birds, fooled by the decoy bird, came down to eat with him and the hunter snared the birds with a noose on a stick.

3. Each buoy was made from a sealskin that was first stretched, dried, and scraped. To make it float, air was blown in and the open ends were tied off.

    Seals themselves were also floated to shore. Fat seals stayed afloat after they were killed, but the skinnier ones tended to sink. The hunters cut slits in such a seal's skin and loosened the blubber with a long curved rod; then they blew air into the opening and plugged the slits with special wooden wound plugs. This made the thinnest seal buoyant!

4. The people on the beach would grab the tow lines and help drag the whale ashore, where it would be greeted with joy and ritual:

    " 'Oh, noble lady, welcome to our village. We have been waiting long for you to honor us with your visit. I bring you sweet water and sacred food.' So saying she dashed a cup of fresh water on the dead whale's muzzle, and then sprinkled a handful of sacred eagle down on it."

    —"Mokwina and the Noble Lady,"
    Page 42, *Cultures of the North Pacific Coast*, Philip Drucker

5. Tules are thick reeds that grow in clumps around inland bodies of water. Each reed is round, tall (16 to 18 feet) and pithy, filled with tiny air pockets. Tules are lightweight and float easily on water.

6. Trees were felled by driving a chiseling tool into the bark. Then a slow-burning fire was set beneath the cut and the charred wood was removed with an adze.

7. A thwart is a board or a brace extending across a boat.

8. Some iron blades were used long before the Europeans came to the Pacific coast. They may have come from an Iron Age settlement in Siberia by way of trade across the Bering Strait. The Japanese current sometimes washed ashore debris from shipwrecks—a hinge or a nail may have become the blade for a Native American adze! Just exactly how iron came to these coasts remains a mystery to this day.

TRADE

Trading was important to the Pacific Coast peoples as it gave each group a chance to get what it didn't have locally, and to pass on its own surplus.

Goods and people traveled along old trading trails that connected tribes to one another and to people far away. Middlemen passed trade objects along, getting something from one trader and exchanging it with another. A Mojave middleman, for example, would get pottery from Arizona people and trade it to a coastal tribe in southern California!

MONEY

Tribes in California used ground clamshell beads (made by the Pomo and Chumash) and pink and gold magnesite beads (ground by the Maidu) as "money."

There were several kinds of such "trade money," but the one valued most by *all* the Pacific Coastal peoples was dentalium shells.

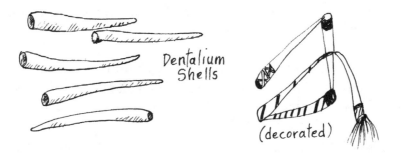

Dentalium Shells

(decorated)

Dentalium Shells

The Kwakiutl people (of today's British Columbia) gathered these slender white shells and traded them with their neighbors. These little tooth-like shells grew in value the further south they were taken!

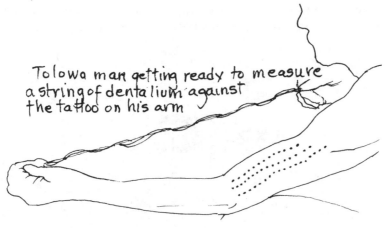

Tolowa man getting ready to measure a string of dentalium against the tattoo on his arm

84

To be used as money a dentalium shell had to be 1 ⁷/₈ inches or longer. It is known that Yurok traders would have tattoos on their upper arms with which they measured the length of a dentalium shell to make sure that it was real money![1]

TRADE ROUTES AND TRAVEL

When California tribes got together to trade, they called it a Gathering—or a Big Time! They traveled along ancient trails that went by water holes and fresh water springs, connecting village to village.

Trading trails ran from San Francisco to San Diego along the coast and around the mountains. Others went along the San Joaquin River through the Central Valley and across Yokut lands. West to east routes crossed the coastal ranges, making it possible to go from the Pacific Ocean to the inland valleys and beyond, through the main passes of the Sierra Nevada, to Nevada's Great Basin!

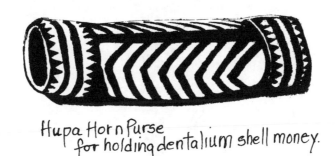

Hupa Horn Purse for holding dentalium shell money.

In the Northwest the Columbia River was used as part of a trade route with the Plains Indians. The coastal tribes of Washington were on one side of the lower river and the peoples of Oregon and California were on the other. It was at Dalles Rapids—where canoes had to be carried overland to calm waters—that the Chinooks held a bustling marketplace! Here people who had different home languages talked to one another in "Chinook Wawa," a trade language.

People throughout the Pacific Coast states enjoyed going on trading trips and their "visits" could last for months.[2] The Makahs, for example, packed their whole families into their huge seagoing canoes and sailed along the coasts, stopping at villages and "trade fairs" as they went.

Such trading times could be serious and ceremonial; feasting and gambling took place as well. It was an opportunity to look at, and trade for, new styles and inventions coming from places as far away as southern California and Alaska.

There was also a trade in "human goods": women, children, and a few men—who had been taken from poor, weak tribes to be used as slaves. They were considered valuable among some Northwest tribes, not so much as a labor source but rather as a symbol of wealth and high standing. (See **Social Groups and Government**.)

The Tlingits of southeast Alaska traveled by sea in their redwood dugouts to trade their sea otter pelts, woven blankets, and copper collected from the Copper River, in exchange for shell ornaments and slaves.

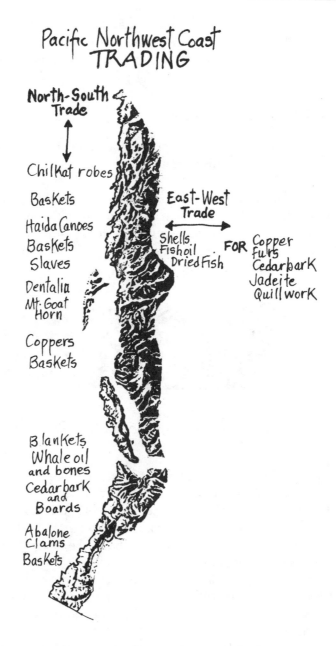

Pacific Northwest Coast
TRADING

North-South Trade

Chilkat robes

Baskets

Haida Canoes
Baskets
Slaves

Dentalia
Mt. Goat Horn

Coppers

Baskets

East-West Trade

Shells,
Fishoil
DriedFish   FOR   Copper
                   Furs
                   Cedarbark
                   Jadeite
                   Quillwork

Blankets
Whale oil
and bones
Cedarbark
and
Boards

Abalone
Clams
Baskets

The Alaskan Yupik traded across the Bering Strait with their cousins, the Siberian Yupik, exchanging Alaskan craft objects and dried meat for spotted reindeer skins and, perhaps, iron. In this way objects from Asia found their way to North America.

Notes for "Trade":

1. Among the Yurok, objects and even *actions* had an exact price in terms of dentalium shell strings, a value that was spelled out in a detailed legal code. For example:

   A piece of land with acorn-bearing oaks on it = 1 to 5 strings

   A fishing spot, depending on how good it was = 1 to 3 strings

   A building, a home = 3 strings

   A slave = 1 to 2 strings

   Killing an important man, whether intentionally or accidentally, regardless of the guilty person's age, gender, or past record = 15 strings

   Killing an unimportant man = 10 strings

2. The Aleuts, it seems, were an exception. They kept mostly to themselves and traded mainly with people from other Aleutian villages. Such trading usually happened in the dead of winter, in December, at a feast or masked dance.

LANGUAGE

TRIBAL LANGUAGES

California

The first Europeans who came to California were amazed at how many languages were spoken there—nearly 100 languages and 300 dialects! Scientists have traced these to six original language "families": Hokan, Yukian, Penutian, Algonquian, Uto-Aztecan, and some Athabascan.[1] Over thousands of years, as the original tribal groups split into small bands and settled away from each other, the languages grew apart.

▲▲▲▲▲▲▲▲

Here are some "Mission Indian" words, spoken among various tribes that had been brought together by Franciscan priests in about 1769; many of these words have a basis in Shoshone, a Uto-Aztecan language.

Woot-chah	sky
Too-kah	sun
Loo-hoh-lo	rain
Too-toh-sah	wind
May-may-ahch	thunder
Koh-hoh-lay	evening
Koh-mah	moon
Hay-see-koh-mah	(big) star
Tchah-kay-hay	springtime
How-nah	morning
Toh-yoh	arrow

Oregon and Washington

The early peoples of the Pacific Northwest spoke languages belonging to the following language families: Algonquian, Athabascan, Hokan-Sioux, Penutian, and Salish.

Inland peoples of the Northwest spoke Uto-Aztecan, Salish, and Shahaptian languages.

Here are a few words in Yakima:

Yoo'-ha	beaver
Lal-la'-wish	wolf
Ah'-mahsh	owl
Yah'-mahsh	deer

| Hahs'-loo | star |
| Tee' chahm | earth |

. . . in Shoshoni:

Tigh-pay	sun
Pah-ah	water
Tahw-ahcahn	dentalia shells
Har-neetz	beaver

. . . and in Nez Perce:

Hah-tee-yah	wind
Tee'-lee-pay	fox
Wee'-tah-loo	dove

Important Languages of the Northwest Coast

1. Eyak
2. Tlingit
3. Haida
4. Makah
5. S. Coast Salish
6. S.W. Coast Salish
7. Chinookans
8. Tillamook
9. Athapaskan
10. Takelma

Alaska

The coastal peoples of the Alaskan Arctic regions spoke languages of the Eskimo-Aleut family, including Aleut, Inuit-Inupiat, and Yupik.

Here are some Inuit words:

Aivik	walrus
Baidarka	a two-hatch kayak
Umialik	owner of a whale hunting boat
Yua	the spirit of an object that has taken a human shape
Igloo (iġdlu)	house
Igluvigaq	*snow* house[2]
Promy shlenniki	Russian fur traders
Puiji	"those who show their noses above the water" (meaning air-breathing sea animals, such as seals)
Tunraq	guardian spirit that helped a shaman with his efforts

Languages from the great Na-Dene family (Athapaskan, Tlingit, and Haida) are spoken in inland and southernmost Alaska.

Words Having to Do with Alaska   *Alaska* is the way Russians pronounced the Aleutian word "Alakshak" which means a peninsula, or great lands, or land that is not an island.

Arctic comes from the Greek words "arkios," meaning northern, and "Arkikos," the Bear, the huge constellation that dominates the northern skies.

Scrimshaw comes from the Old English word "scrymshank": to fool around, to avoid regular work.

The Inupiat (North Eskimo) Months of the Year   This calendar shows how important the seasons were to the Inupiat's life. Included are some other Inuit expressions for the same months.

January	siqinyasak tatqiq	moon of the returning sun
February	izrasuġruk tatqiq	coldest moon
March	paniqsiksiivik tatqiq	moon for bleaching skins
April	aġaviksiuvik tatqiq (Inuit)	moon for beginning whaling little birds come, owls come
May	suvluraviq tatqiq	moon when rivers flow
June	irniivik tatqiq	moon when animals give birth
July	inyukuksaivik tatqiq	moon when birds raise their young
August	aqavirvik tatqiq (Inuit)	moon when birds molt geese cannot fly
September	tingiivik tatqiq	moon when birds fly south
October	nuliavik tatqiq (Inuit)	moon when caribou rut sewing moon, shamans get busy
November	nippiviq tatqiq	moon of the setting sun
December	siqinrilak tatqiq (Inuit)	moon with no sun they shine (the evening stars)

INUIT POEMS

Delight in Singing

*It's wonderful
to make up song:
but all too many of them fail.*

*It's wonderful
to have your wishes granted;
but all too often
they slip by.*

*It's wonderful
to hunt reindeer:
but all too seldom
you succeed,
standing like a bright fire
on the plain.*

—Piuvkaq

Polar Bear

*I saw a polar bear
on an ice-drift.
He seemed harmless as a dog,
who comes running towards you,
wagging his tail.
But so much
did he want to get at me
that when I jumped aside
he went spinning on the ice.
We played this game of tag
from morning until dusk.
But then, at last, I tired him out,
and ran my spear into his side.*

—Aua

Reindeer

I wriggled silently through the swamp,
carrying bow and arrow in my mouth.
The marsh was broad, the water icy cold,
and there was no cover in sight.

I crawled within range.
The reindeer were eating;
they grazed the juicy moss
without concern,
till my arrow sank
tremblingly deep
into the bull's side.

Terrified, the unsuspecting herd
hastily scattered,
and vanished at the sharpest trot
to shielding hills.

—Aua

The Mother's Song

It is so still in the house.
There is a calm in the house;
The snowstorm wails out there.
And the dogs are rolled up with snouts under the tail.
My little boy is sleeping on the ledge,
On his back he lies, breathing through his open mouth.
His little stomach is bulging round —
Is it strange if I start to cry with joy?

—An Arctic Eskimo Poem

Moved

(A song that would always send the shaman Uvavnuk into a trance)

The great sea stirs me.
The great sea sets me adrift,
it sways me like the weed
on a river-stone.
The sky's height stirs me.
The strong wind blows through my mind.
It carries me with it,
so I shake with joy.

—Uvavnuk

Untitled

When I was young,
every day was as a beginning
of some new thing.
And every evening ended
with the glow of the next day's dawn.

—*An Arctic Eskimo Poem*

RIDDLES

Riddling was a playful pastime and, after a good guess, the Alaskan riddler would say, "HA HU!" ("Good guess" or "good try!").

California

What is always happy to stick its head in the fire? (**a log**)
What rushes down the hillside flashing like fire? (**a red fox's tail**)
What three things should not be touched? (**a briar bush, poison oak, a thorny stem**)

The Northwest

What animal drags his shovel along the trail? (**a beaver**)
What has feathers and can sail through the air but is not a bird? (**an arrow**)
What flies up ringing a tiny bell? (**a mosquito**)

Alaska

I cannot play but I make others play. What am I? (**a ball**)
In the spring what looks like a herd of deer lying down? (**bare spots of ground where the snow has melted on a frozen hillside**)
Four fingers and a thumb, yet flesh and bones, have I none. What am I? (**a leather glove**)
Big as an igloo, light as a feather, yet 40 dogs can't pull it. What is it? (**the shadow of an igloo**)
Tell me this: In many ways I'm like a broom, I sweep clean all around me. (**the tops of grasses when the wind blows across the snow**)
I see two shining lakes, one beside the other. (**a hunter's eyes on a windy day**)
Wait, they sound like pretty little songs being sung to children of the next world. (**a fast-moving stream and waterfall**)
Tell me this: I see many little shining nests and soon they disappear. (**the small whirlpools made by a canoe's paddle**)
Wait: a hand comes down and covers the world. (**nightfall and darkness**)
Wait: a singer is coming—and now he isn't. ((**a short gust of wind**)

*I see many little brothers chasing each other, higher and higher they go until they disappear in the night. (**sparks flying up from the fire in the dark**)*

*Tell me: We come upstream, many of us in flash-red canoes. (**salmon at spawning time**)*

*Like a stand of pine trees after a fire. (**the walrus' black whiskers**)*

*It flies straight ahead, always pressing its head against the air. (**a bird point or arrow head**)*

PETROGLYPHS AND PICTOGRAPHS

Petroglyphs are rock pictures made by *carving* lines into stone surfaces. They are found throughout the United States, including California, Oregon, and Washington. (There are, in fact, over 600 petroglyph sites just from northern California to southwestern Alaska.) Scientists date such rock pictures as having been carved from about 1500 B.C. to about A.D. 1800.

Pictographs are pictures made by *painting* on rock surfaces with natural pigments made of ground rocks and earth (yellow ochre, brown, tan), clay (red and white), and charcoal (black). Ancient pictographs protected from the wind, rain, and snow (by overhanging cliffs or inside caves) have lasted to be seen by us today.

Why did the early peoples make this rock art? Of course, we cannot be certain but it seems that they were meant to act like language: they were meant to give information. People who study rock pictures and paintings have several ideas about what they mean; which ones do you find convincing? Petroglyphs and pictographs may have been:

- prayers to spirits or guardian animals
- a permanent record of a person's Vision Quest
- a way to teach young children about the world of the spirits
- information about the place; e.g., where to find water nearby
- a record of events that took place there; e.g., a battle

It took considerable time to carve a rock picture, so its "message" must have been important to its creator. In the state of Washington many petroglyphs are found that show eyes staring back at the viewer. What can we make of these?

STORYTELLING

Why the Tales Were Told

Stories often taught geography, history, and nature. Tales might be shared with young people as they learned sewing, beading, basketry, or tanning—entertaining and distracting the youngsters while they did these repetitive tasks. Tales also taught important community values.

> "My parents, uncles and granduncles told me in days gone by, stories which would create in me the desire to be brave, and good, and strong, to become a good speaker, a good leader. They taught me to honor old people and always do all in my power to help them. The old Indian way was to teach through stories."
>
> —Chief William Shelton, Snohomish

To the early people nothing was inanimate. Animals, plants, rocks, water, manmade objects—*all* natural things—were fully alive with complicated and rich histories, and capable of thinking and causing things to happen.

Among some Californians the story itself was thought to be alive. The storyteller was only allowed to call it up at night in the winter; otherwise, he or she would be made a hunchback or bitten by rattlesnakes—and there would be bad luck for everyone. Since the story had its own mind, it, like all things, had to be treated with respect.

The fact that various California tribes explained the world's creation differently in their stories did not seem to trouble them. Their reaction was to say: "This is how we tell it. They tell it another way."

Finally, tales were told to engage you, to make you laugh or sigh as a group, to make you feel the force of family. Stories made you wonder at being alive in this world.

Story Knives

Ivory story knives were an important part of Eskimo wintertime storytelling. The Inuit storyteller acted out the different roles and, as the tale unfolded, he or she used the knife to draw scenes in the snow to illustrate the tale.

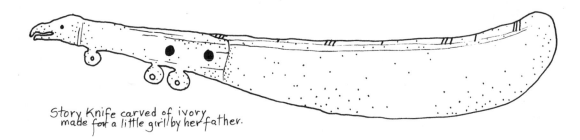

Story Knife carved of ivory made for a little girl by her father.

13 NATIVE AMERICAN TALES OF THE COASTAL INDIANS

California

The Little Acorn Girls (Karuk)

Once acorns were all Spirit people (Ikxareyavs). Then one day they heard a voice say, "You will soon be leaving this Spirit World, so you will all need good hats to wear down there in the Karuk world." So they started to weave some very pretty hats.

Then the voice said, "You've got to leave right *now*. The people are being made down in the Karuk world! Hurry, hurry, go down right NOW!"

Well, Tan Oak Acorn didn't get a chance to clean her hat and smooth it out. Black Oak Acorn didn't have time to even finish *weaving* her hat, so she just picked up a bowl basket and put it on her head. But both Maul Oak Acorn and Post Oak Acorn finished *their* hats and these hats were perfect in every way!

When Tan Oak Acorn saw those beautiful hats, she said, "Maybe my hat is not as smooth as theirs but I bet *I* will make the best acorn *soup*!"

Then all the little Acorn Girls went down to earth. They spilled from the heavens right down into the land of the Karuk. "These people are just going to LOVE us," they said. They were really all Ikxareyavs, those little Acorn girls. And as they fell to earth they each covered their face with their hat.

When Black Oak Acorn hit the ground, she became striped—and if you pick her up even today, she's still striped. Tan Oak Acorn didn't paint herself much 'cause she was still mad about not getting to finish her hat—she was *also* grumpy with Tan Oak and Maul Oak Acorn when she saw their beautiful hats, so she wished them bad luck. And they *got* it: even to this day no one wants to eat Post Oak or Maul Oak Acorns because they taste bad and they will make your soup black!

So it was when the Ikxareyavs spilled down to earth: they covered their faces with their hats. And when you look at them all today, you'll see they *still* have covered their faces with their little woven hats!

Black Oak Acorn

Tan Oak Acorn

Maul Oak Acorn

The Girl Who Married a Rattlesnake (Pomo)

Once there was a Pomo village and in it were four big houses. One of these houses had a center pole and in this house there lived a girl.

She was graceful, kind, and hard working and there lived a rattlesnake nearby who noticed this girl so that one day he followed her. Outside her house the snake changed himself into a handsome young man with a winning smile. He climbed onto the roof, slid down the pole, and set out to win the young girl's heart. Four days he came in the afternoon and left the next morning. Four days he pleased the girl AND her parents. Then on the fifth day the rattlesnake did not change himself into a human, but rather he slithered into the house as the snake he really was. Once inside he began speaking just as ever and the girl's mother heard him and she took a light and walked toward the voice— there she saw the rattlesnake and she dropped the light and screamed. And the rattlesnake stayed the whole night.

In the morning the snake took the girl home with him. There she stayed and in time she gave him four sons. Whenever one of her children saw a human, he would coil to strike but his mother would say, "Stop, you mustn't bite a relative!"

After a time the rattlesnake boys said, "You're not like us, are you, Mother?"

"No, I am not a serpent."

"Why aren't you afraid of Father then?" the boys asked.

"I am not afraid of him because I love him. I am still a human but I feel myself changing so I need to go back to my village and see my parents one last time."

Her parents were sad to hear that she would not come to see them again. They talked together a long time. When the visit was over, the girl's mother went up to her and held her firmly so she could *not* leave. But the girl shook herself and suddenly she was gone, never to be seen again. Where could she have gone...back to her rattlesnake love?

Coyote and the Bullhead (Wintu)

Coyote was walkin' along the river on his way to a party. He was all dressed up wearin' his finest moccasins, a beaded loincloth, lots of necklaces, and his good quiver filled with bow and arrows. Well, he stopped by the water and he saw Bullhead, all black and shiny, sunning himself near shore. "What'cha doin' in there?" said Coyote.

The fish said nothin'! "You sure are a little guy," continued Coyote, and he nudged Bullhead with his foot. "I bet you couldn't even swallow my *toe*!" and Coyote wiggled his toes by Bullhead, but the fish just turned his head away. Coyote kept on teasin' and botherin' Bullhead for a very long time, insultin' him, tryin' to make the black fish mad.

At last, Bullhead grabbed Coyote's toe and he swallowed it! Coyote hardly noticed and kept on teasin' him. So Bullhead swallowed his ankle and then his leg. . . . NOW Coyote got worried and he begged the Bullhead to give him back his foot and leg. "I'll give you my beads and my quiver and my bow and arrows!" But no, that ol' fish kept on swallowing Coyote. "O.K., O.K., I'll give you my moccasins and my breech cloth!" But it was too late; Bullhead swallowed Coyote completely and then went and laid under a rock.

Well, time passed. The people all said, "Where's Coyote? Where is that ol' rascal?" Some of 'em went down to the river and they saw where he'd been dragged into the water. So they asked a medicine man to help 'em find Coyote. The medicine man went into a trance and he said, "Bullhead swallowed Coyote and he ain't dead yet."

Bullhead knew they were lookin' for him so he used his tail to muddy the water: not even Raccoon or Otter could see him. But high up in a tree sat a bird, Mud Spear, and she said, "I see Bullhead muddying the water and I'll dive down and spear him so we can save Coyote!" She dived down and speared the fish and they cut it open and out jumped Coyote! "Wow, I was takin' a little nap and you woke me UP!" was all he said and off he trotted down the path, still on his way to the party!

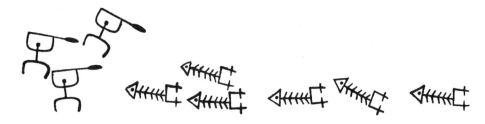

In the Land of the Dead (SERRANO)

Once long ago a great hunter brought home a new wife. His mother didn't like her and, first chance she got, she hid a poisoned thorn in the young woman's cushion so when she sat down, the young wife died.

The people of the tribe made a huge pile of brush; they set it on fire and laid her body on it. All day it burned so when the husband came home that night, nothing was left but ashes.

Well, he stayed there by the smoldering coals and did not leave; the smoke and ashes rose up and swirled off like a column down the road. The husband followed the pillar of smoke and in a while he realized that it was his young wife.

"I am going to the Land of the Dead," she said. "Come get on my back and I will take you with me." And so he did and they went into the Land of the Dead and right up to her people. Then they met her father and mother and young sisters and uncles and cousins—all the ones from her life who had died.

Now some of the Dead felt awkward toward the young hunter because he was still alive, but his wife pleaded for him so he was allowed to stay.

It was an odd life there—no one woke up during the day as the dead only came out at night. And he didn't eat their food so he had to find his own. One night they said they were going hunting and asked him to come with them and stay in one spot by the trail. He stayed there and after a while he heard the Dead yelling, "Deer! Deer!" and the man looked around...and he didn't see any deer—the only things he saw were two black beetles ambling down the trail and he pushed them over. When the Dead came up, they praised him as a truly great hunter for those were *their* deer—those *beetles*!, and from then on he often helped them on their hunts.

Now time passed and the man got thin and the Dead told his wife: "This is hard for him, being here. You should go off with him and you can, if once you get back there you don't touch each other for three whole days"; but sad to say, three days for the Dead meant three years for the living. . . .

So the hunter and his wife returned to their camp and the whole tribe rejoiced. There was lots of feasting and for three whole days the husband did not touch his young wife. The fourth night they had laid down to go to sleep and they were so happy that they hugged each other. In the morning, when he awoke, the great hunter was alone once more.

Pacific Northwest

The Origin Story of the Yakimas

In the beginning all was water. The Great Chief above lived in the sky all by himself. He grew lonely and so he went below. There in the shallows he dug up mud and he tossed it to one side, making land. In some places the mud piled high and these were the first mountains. When it rained the snow and ice began to cover the mountaintops.

The Great Chief made trees, roots, and berries. He filled the land with deer, rabbits, and bear. He filled the waters with fish. Then he took a ball of mud and made man. And when this man grew lonely, the Great Chief made a woman to be his friend. He taught her how to clean and to cook the game the man brought home.

Then one night the woman had a dream. In it she asked the Great Chief to show her how to make their life even more happy. The Great Chief then blew on the woman and he gave her a gift. He filled a basket with something she could not see, hear, smell, or touch; but from then on she understood how to weave and how to make pottery and which designs should go on each. These things she taught her children and they taught theirs.

In time the Great Chief made other men and women. But after a while they began fighting. This angered Mother Earth and she shook the land so hard that the mountains above Big River fell down and filled the canyon and killed many. Someday the Great Chief above will turn over these mountains and set free the spirits trapped below; but only the spirits of those who fell, not the ones who were fighting.

We did not know all this. We were told by our fathers and our grandfathers. Everything is just as they said. When you are out in the mountains looking for plants and animals, you can tell that this story is true.

Lifting the Sky (SNOHOMISH)

In the beginning the Creator made the world. He started at the east and came on west. Each place he went he made people and gave them a language. When he got to northern Washington, the Creator stopped. "I like this place so much that I'm not goin' any farther," he said. "I've got a *lot* of languages left, but that's okay. I'll just sprinkle them around all over here." And he did. That's why today there are so very many different languages in this place.

Well, back in those days the sky was very low. Tall people were always bumping their heads on it and that didn't feel good at all. The wise elders talked it over and decided that *everybody*—the peoples and all the animals—should get together and use really tall poles to try to lift up the sky.

This was a fine idea but the people needed a way to know *when* everybody should lift up on their poles.

"Once we're all ready, we need the elders to yell out 'YA-HOH!' so all of us can lift up on our poles together." (It was lucky for them that "Ya-Hoh" meant "lift together" in all of their languages!)

So then the birds and the people and the animals got their long poles and they all came together.

When everybody was ready, the elders yelled out "YA-HOH!" and every creature raised its pole at one time . . . and the sky was lifted up too. They had to do this a few more times but it worked because the sky was high overhead—just as it is today!

Now I've gotta' tell you there were a few creatures on that day who hadn't known about the sky lifting and this is what happened to them:

Four friends were out in two canoes fishing. When the sky was lifted, they were tossed up into the Sky World and their fish went along with them! At that same moment, three hunters were stalking elk at a place where the ground almost met the sky. The four elk jumped up into the Sky World and the hunters and their dog ran after them.

In the Sky World they all got changed to stars and that's how they've stayed. The three hunters are the handle of the Big Dipper. The middle hunter has his dog with him . . . and it is now a tiny star.

The Pacific Northwest people still shout *Ya-Hoh!* whenever they lift something heavy. Their voices go so high on the end of the word and they make the "Hoh" last a long time. That's how it is today just as it was before.

How We Got Things in the Sky (Makah)

Aurora Borealis   Many moons' journey to the North lives a tribe of dwarf Indians, each only three feet tall. Although they are small they are extremely strong and able to dive into the freezing waters—and they catch whales using only their hands. Then they build fires on the ice and boil the blubber. These fires make those lights you sometimes see in the North skies at night. The Aurora Borealis? It's the tiny people boiling their whale meat way up North.

Rainbow   It was the Thunderbird who put the rainbow in the sky. At each end there are powerful claws. Don't try to get close to a rainbow or you will end up in those claws.

Comet, Meteor   Each comet, each meteor, is the spirit of some now departed chief. Every star is the spirit of a person or an animal, bird, snake, or fish that once lived on this earth.

Thunder   Thunderbird is a giant Indian who lives on top of the highest mountain. When he gets hungry, he puts on the head and wings of a huge bird, covers his body with feathers, and ties lightning fish around his waist. Thunderbird flies down to the sea and his wings make huge rumblings as they darken the sky. When he sees a whale, he throws the lightning fish at it and the whale gets killed. Then he carries the dead whale back to the mountain where he eats it.

A Mother's Promise
(A Chomawi creation story by Rosemary Sabbas, as told by her grandmother)

In the very beginning there was nothing but water. There were two Creators— Coyote and Silver Fox—and they needed each other. Then they became humans. That means they can think; they think themselves a boat. They float around on the water in the boat. They float and they float. When they get tired of doing that, Silver Fox puts Coyote to sleep.

While Coyote's sleeping, Silver Fox starts brushing Coyote's hair. He brushes. He brushes. Then he takes the fur that he gets out of the brush and Silver Fox pats it. He rolls it. He pats and pulls and presses it until he makes the earth and he sets it off a ways from them. Then he takes four stones and weighs it down so it won't drift off.

After some time their boat floats up to the edge of the earth. That wakes Coyote up! He looks at the earth and says, "What in the world? . . . Where did it come from?"

"How would *I* know?" says Silver Fox. "We just got here!"

They get out of their boat. They go up the hill. They make a sweat lodge and live together.

Alaska

Raven Brings Back the Light
(This story is also told in the Pacific Northwest)

In the very beginning the earth was young and in twilight. The Chief of the Sky gave a black Raven suit to one of the young men who lived in the heavens with him. The boy put on the feather suit and flew down to earth. There he saw how the people were all stumbling around in the near darkness. He thought, "I want to bring some of the light of heaven down here to the earth."

So Raven flew back up into the skies, changed himself into a cedar needle, and dropped into the village spring. When the Sky Chief's daughter came down to get a drink of fresh water, Raven went right into her dipper and she drank the cedar needle without even knowing it.

Soon the girl began to grow fat and it wasn't long before she had a baby—Raven. Her little boy looked like a human baby except for his nose which WAS very pointed. . . . Nobody could believe how fast this baby grew—and how *smart* he was. The Sky Chief adored his new grandson and would do ANYTHING for him—except let him play with the glow of daylight which he kept in his lodge in a box.

But the little boy cried and cried and nagged and nagged until at last the Chief let him play with the magic box. "Watch him now," said the Chief, "don't let him open that box."

Well, the minute no one was watching, Raven baby put on the feather suit and with the box under his wing, he flew down to the world. Raven lighted in a tree near a river. He looked down and saw the men fishing in the dim light and he asked them to please bring him a fish. But the men pretended not to hear him. This made Raven furious and he threw the carved magic box down onto the rocks below.

There was a blinding glare of light! And all at once dawn came—and so it has been right up to this day!

Origin Myth (INUIT)

There was another world before this one but the pillars that held it up became weak. When they crumbled, the world disappeared and then there was nothing. No earth. No light. No Inuit.

Out of a little mound of mud came two men. They were born and they were grown all at once. But they wanted children and they didn't get any until a magic song was sung and it changed one of the men into a woman and very soon after this children came into the world. All of these were the first Inuits.

First Man's Disappointment (INUIT)

One day First Man went out to hunt. He was hungry. His wife was hungry and so were his son and daughter-in-law. Then First Man sighted a seal. He silently crept up on it but it slid into the sea. Then he spotted a second seal and this time he crawled toward it without a sound, but the animal jumped into the water and was gone. All day long, one after another, the seals *all* escaped him! As the sun went down, First Man turned back toward his home. His chest felt very tight within him; his throat ached. Then he felt water coming down his face and First Man threw back his head and a strange long howl came from him.

When he reached home, his family came to meet him. They saw the water coming down his face. They heard the strange sounds he was making.

"Where is our meat, O Father?" they asked.

"Gone. All gone. There is no food tonight for any of us." And hearing this his family all were taken with the same sickness and they began to wail along with First Man. And this is how the Inuits first learned how to cry.

The Myth of Sedna (INUIT)

Sedna and her father lived alone by the sea. She had grown into a beautiful woman and many an Inuit hunter came to ask that she join him as his wife. But not one of them touched her heart. Then one day a seagull, called a fulmar, came down and landed next to the young beauty.

"Oh, Sedna," it pleaded in its soft honeyed voice, "come live with me in the land of the birds. There you shall have a splendid tent furnished with the softest bear skins. You will never need to work and *anything* you wish will be yours!"

Sedna was completely taken by the fulmar's charms and together they traveled to the other end of the world, to the land of the birds.

Ah, Sedna, her life was not as the fulmar had promised: her tent was made of rotten fish skins, the furs she slept on were hard old walrus hides. The only food she had was tiny minnows which the birds dropped outside her tent.

She was so miserable that she sang "Aja, O Father, come get me. I am so badly treated here. O come take me home, dear Father! Aja!"

Far off to the North her father heard Sedna's song and he paddled all the way to the other end of the world. Once in the land of the birds, her father was outraged to find his child in such a disastrous place and in his outrage he struck and killed the fulmar. Then he took Sedna and they fled in his boat.

When the fulmars found the dead husband, they were very sad. They began searching for his runaway wife. They cried out over the death of their friend and they still mourn and cry to this very day.

The fulmars flew over the waters of the sea and when they saw Sedna's boat below, they caused a huge storm to arise. Waves towered over the boat and the father grew frenzied with fear. "Why should we *both* die? It's YOU they want!" he cried, and he flung his daughter into the sea. But Sedna hung onto the side of his boat. So the father took his knife and cut off all the first joints of her fingers. They fell into the water and became whales and the nails became walruses. Still Sedna held on. So her father cut off the second finger joints and these swam off as seals. The crazed man now chopped off the finger stumps which turned into smaller seals and only then did Sedna fall into the water and go to the bottom of the sea. There she lives to this day with all her children—the whales, seals, and walruses—all about her.

Inuit hunters call her the Great Woman and, when hunting is poor, they believe she is withholding the animals from them. Then a hunter will cry out, "Sedna, please share the creatures of the sea with this poor man," and often she may.

How We Got Mosquitoes (TLINGIT)

Once there was a huge giant who lived only to kill people, eat their flesh, and drink their blood.

At last the people got together to talk it over.

"I think I know how to get rid of this giant," said one man.

"Okay, go try," they told him.

So, the man went down the road that the giant often used and he laid down on the dirt. Soon the giant came along. He was overjoyed to find a fresh warm human and he took the man back to his house. Once in the kitchen the giant saw that he was out of firewood so he went out to get some. While the giant was out, the man jumped up and grabbed a butcher knife . . . just as the giant's little son came in. The man grabbed the young giant and put the knife to his throat.

"Tell me how I can stab your father in the heart," said the man.

The giant's son was scared. He swallowed and then he said, "The giant's heart is in his left heel!" The man let him go and then the man hid.

When the giant came back into the kitchen, the man jumped out and stabbed him in the heel and the giant keeled over. With his last breath he whispered, "You may have killed me, but I'm going to keep on eating you humans forever!"

"No way," said the man and he cut up the dead giant's body and burnt it all in the fireplace. When the ashes cooled, he took them out and threw them into the wind.

Ah, but the cloud of ashes became a swarm of *mosquitoes*! . . . With a heavy whining they covered the man and each mosquito began sucking his blood. When they had finished, the man began to itch and scratch. That's how it was. . . . That's how it will be until the end of this world!

Notes for "Language":

1. The languages are listed here in the order that the original speakers are thought to have arrived in California. Languages from these same families were spoken in many other parts of the continent. For example, Zuni, spoken in New Mexico, is a Penutian language and Algonquian was (and is) spoken on the Atlantic Coast of the U.S. and Canada.

2. Often it has been said that the Eskimos have hundreds of words for snow. How many words for it do they actually have? The language of the Yupik Eskimos, in particular, has some two dozen roots describing snow or things related to snow. It turns out that the English language has about the same number; for example: snow, sleet, slush, blizzard, avalanche, powder, hardpack, snowflake, snowfall, snowball, snowman, and so on.

   The Eskimo languages can form hundreds of words from a single root, so it *is* true that the total of snow-based words could be large. But this is true of *all* nouns in their languages, not just snow.

ARTS AND CRAFTS

To the Native American art was not a separate thing in life, art was *everything* they made; the tiny decorations that Alaskans made on clothing to be worn *inside* other clothes are an example of this way of thinking.

MUSIC

Singing

Singing—whether individually or as a group, spontaneous or ceremonial—was very important. Songs were medicine, tools to be used in healing, hunting, or the making of objects. Songs could help you get love, success in war, and protection from harm.

The Inuits used songs to call a whale or walrus to come meet their harpoons; they sang in sorrow, in praise, to ridicule, and to celebrate being alive.

How the Coastal Native Americans Got Their Songs

The music of early peoples comes from deep in Myth Time; Coyote, Grizzly Bear, Mountain Lion, and Peregrine Falcon all left their songs to the Northwest people. Often personal songs were gotten on vision quests, or when visiting a sacred place; these songs came to mind in their complete form, received as a gift from the Earth.

Although it was not permitted to sing other persons' songs without their permission, songs were often given—as a man aged—to stronger younger singers.

"I can't sing these songs anymore, the way I used to. No wind left. That's why I don't go around the dances any more. . . . I been thinkin' you boys are pretty good singers. So I decided I'm gonna will my songs to you. So they go on."

—Bill Patterson, speaking to David Tripp and Julian Lang (cousins)
as quoted in *News from Native California*, vol. 4, no. 2, Winter 1990, page 23

Musical Instruments

The California people made rattles from baskets, deer toes, gourds, moth cocoons, or split sticks.

In the Northwest rattles were carved of alder in two pieces that fit neatly together to hold a few pebbles. The round part might be made to look like an animal or a mythical being.

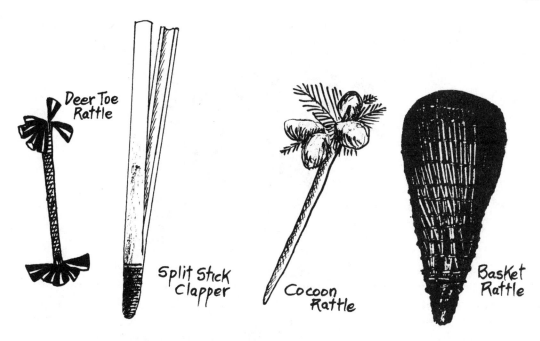

Deer Toe Rattle

Split Stick Clapper

Cocoon Rattle

Basket Rattle

Whistles, flutes, and panpipes were played by all early people. On the south California coast, they were made from soapstone; in other places, from bird bones or reeds. People made music with them but they were also used to call birds, give signals in battle, and sometimes to shock a patient under treatment by a shaman!

Haida Rattle

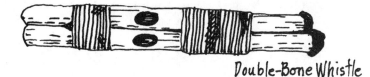

Double-Bone Whistle

Four-Holed Flute

Hide-covered hand drums were made by people of all the West Coast states. An Eskimo used a drumming wand to strike the edges and center of his drum.

In the Northwest the simplest drum used was a wooden plank raised off the ground a bit by two wooden blocks. It was played with hardwood sticks. Box drums were built like cooking boxes but were long, narrow, and deep. Such a drum was hung from a roof beam and the drummer sat beside it. His fist was wrapped in shredded cedar bark and, as he pounded the drum with it, deep sounds filled the long house.

Tlingit wooden drum with Killer whale design.

Only one kind of stringed instrument was used in the Pacific coast states: it was a simple musical bow played by just a few California tribes! It was modeled after a hunting bow. One end was held in the mouth while the string was tapped making lovely soft sounds.

VISUAL ARTS

Basketry

Outstanding baskets were woven by many California groups. They were shaped and decorated in different ways depending on the tribe and the use. Some Pomo storage baskets were large enough for a man to stand in.

"The Mission Indians" often wove two intertwining star shapes into their baskets. Tribes in the southern Central Valley made baskets called Tulares, which sometimes had a rattlesnake pattern. The Yokuts made "friendship baskets" that showed figures holding hands. An example is illustrated below.

Yokut Friendship Basket

Northwest and Alaskan basket makers also wove baby carriers, cradleboards, and containers for personal effects. Baskets were made with local materials such as grasses and red cedar or spruce roots, most often using the techniques of coiling or twining.

These same people used designs that showed landscapes, animals, and even whaling scenes—as among the Makah—and decorated the baskets with painting, feathers, fur, and beads.

Pomo Feathered Basket

Weaving

Blankets were woven in the colder areas, north of California. Mountain goat wool was mixed with dog hair (from a special breed raised in northernmost Washington), or down from waterfowl, or milkweed and/or fluffy cattails. The goat wool was beaten with fine white clay to take out excess oils. Then the animal and plant fibers were combed with the fingers and spun into yarn.

The Salish used a full two-bar loom. The Tlingit (and other tribes nearby) wove blankets on a half-loom with a single bar holding up the hanging warp strands.

Woven matting made from ribbons of bark was used for bedding, partitions, floor coverings, and capes. Such matting could be plain, painted, or have a checkerboard pattern. In prehistoric times these mats were used as sails and, at the end of a person's life, as a shroud.

BEAR WITH YOUNG   Chilkat Blanket

Woodworking and Carving

Tools found in early sites show that woodcarving was being done in the Pacific Northwest as far back as 5000 B.C. Woodworking became the main craft in this area and each large group had its own style. Their other crafts—painting, weaving, and carving horn, stone and bone—were all reflections of their work with wood.

The Alaskan people carved (whale)bone, some wood, and ivory. Each object they crafted was a thing of perfection and beauty.

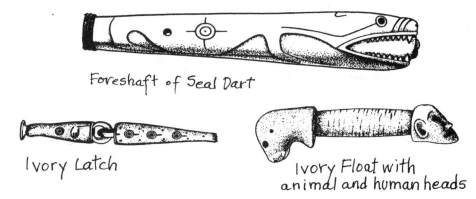

Foreshaft of Seal Dart

Ivory Latch

Ivory Float with animal and human heads

Totem Poles

...covered with figures which might be taken for a species of hierogliphics (*sic*): fishes and other animals, heads of men and various whimsical designs are mingled and confounded in order to compose a subject. It will not be expected that the proportions in these figures be exactly observed; for here every man is a painter and sculptor; yet they are not deficient in a sort of elegance and perfection.

—Captain Étienne Marchand, August 1791

(The totem pole was very important in Northwest culture. Its many roles are described in **Social Groups and Government**.)

The clan chief selected the figure he wanted on the totem pole and commissioned an artist to design it. The people who made the poles had trained as apprentices with a master carver. In early times they used stone, shell, or bone tools.

Red cedar was used for most of the poles; in the north, where it was not always available, yellow (Alaskan) cedar was used instead. The paint was made by mixing natural mineral pigments with a binder made from crushed salmon eggs (roe).

> Once they had been forest trees until the Indian (cut) them and turned them into bare poles. Then he enriched the shorn things with carvings. He wanted some way of showing people things...about the creature and about himself and their relation to each other...birds and animals and fish...he let his imaginings rise above the objects that he saw and pictured supernatural beings too.
>
> —Emily Carr, c. 1886, *Klee Wyth*, page 51

Raising these huge poles required skilled cooperation and was accompanied by a traditional ceremony. Often a hundred men were needed to carry the pole to the site, where a deep trench had been dug leading into the hole in which the pole would be stood. It was laid down in the trench and all the men pulled on a rope tied to its upper end until the pole was standing upright.

In earlier times a pole, once erected, was not removed,[1] even if the people moved their village to another place.

Boxes and Chests   Northwest craftsmen made bentwood boxes and chests so well that these containers were watertight. Then they decorated them, sometimes showing the front of an animal on the face of the box and its hindquarters on the back.[2]

Bentwood Box

Masks   The masks of the Northwest were exceptional in detail, size, and variety. They were carved of wood (or whalebone) and painted, often having inlaid copper or abalone details. Shredded bark was sometimes added for "hair." Making masks with moveable parts was a specialty of the Makah people (and the Kwakaiutl in Canada). By pulling on a string or several cords within the mask, it could be made to open and close its mouth, roll its eyes, or unfurl the feathers on its head. The man who wore the huge Raven Mask made it clack its bill by jerking his neck and mouth.

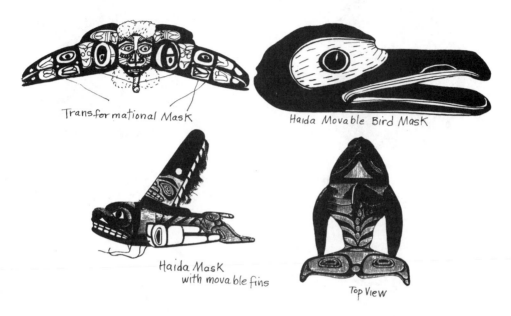

Transformational Mask

Haida Movable Bird Mask

Haida Mask with movable fins

Top View

Southern Alaska Eskimo masks stand out because of their unusual style and form. The face of one of these masks could be surrounded by feathers, or the mask could cover just a part of the face.

Northern Alaska Eskimo masks were carved of heavy whalebone or weathered wood. Alaskan women made finger masks that were worn on the middle and fore fingers, so that they could "talk together" like puppets.

Jewelry

Every culture group adorns itself. The early Pacific coastal people wore earrings of clay, carved bird bone, seashells, or ivory; and necklaces of abalone, shells, ivory, or soapstone beads.

The Californians also wore soapstone ear plugs, abalone pins, hairpins, and breast ornaments (called *gorgets*). Farther north, rings and nose plugs were worn, as well as necklaces made of pine nut beads and braided straw. A popular pendant for a necklace was an elkhorn louse crusher!

Coastal Alaskan natives made necklaces of sea animal teeth and wore labrets (lip plugs) made of shell, ivory, soapstone, or wood. Men often wore two labrets, one at each side of the lower lip; women might wear chin or lip plugs.

Alaskan Eskimo Labrets

Notes for "Arts and Crafts":

1. The "ridicule" pole was an exception. (See **Social Groups and Government**).
2. This is how a Northwest cedar box was made:
   a. A cedar board was cut and adzed to even thickness.
   b. Three grooves (or kerfs) were cut almost through the board. (See Photo 35.)
   c. Each kerf had to be exactly square in cross-section and spaced perfectly so that it could be folded in on itself, making a watertight seal. This was done by steaming the kerf over hot stones in a pit, until the kerf could be bent at a right angle.

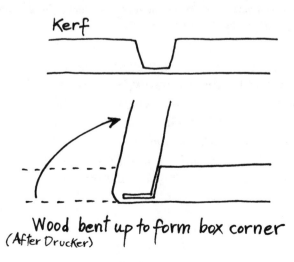

Kerf

Wood bent up to form box corner
(After Drucker)

Photo 35. To make wall and roof boards, Northwest people split planks from living trees. *Photo by E. S. Curtis. Courtesy Santa Barbara Museum of Natural History.*

d. The board ends were cut to form a tight joint and were pegged or sewn together with withes (tough and flexible willow twigs) through drilled holes.

e. A board was cut to the exact size of the joined sides and a flange was cut all around its outside edge. This made a mortised joint and was held together in place with pegs driven into drilled holes.

f. Lids were made by carving a board to fit over the box top, OR by grooving a thick board to fit down on the box top, OR by making a second box to fit completely over the first one!

CHILDREN AND PLAY

NEWBORN BABIES

Newborn babies were welcomed with ceremonies and magic rites to make sure they would have good health and long lives.

When a baby was born in California and the Pacific Northwest, the baby was tightly and thickly wrapped into a basketry cradle carrier. This protected the child from harsh winds—as well as from poisonous plants or snakes. Soft moss covered the baby's bottom; the moss was changed whenever it got wet. In northern Alaska the newborn was wrapped tightly under the mother's parka against her warm back. Such wrapped babies hardly ever fussed or cried.

Many people have wondered how being wrapped tightly from birth might affect and form a child. Did it make the child feel safe and protected? Would it help a baby learn to watch *and* observe what was going on in the world?

The Chinook and Salish gave their babies flattened foreheads which they thought beautiful. This was done by tying a board to a baby's padded skull for the first year of life. (The babies of slaves were not allowed to have this beauty treatment.)

YOUNG CHILDREN

Children learned by watching, listening, and imitating. As the children grew older, their mothers and grandmothers taught them good manners and the right way to act. From songs and stories the children learned about their people's history and community values. In the Northwest, for example, children might hear the clan tales—long histories of the family, full of details about its honor, wealth, and heroes—that taught the basic lessons of clan loyalty and pride.[1]

Both boys and girls were taught that being thrifty, hardworking, brave, and strong should be lifelong goals. Quarreling and causing problems were to be avoided.

The grownups and the older children saw to it that the young ones behaved. Teasing words were used to remind them to do the right thing. Hardly ever was a child hit in order to punish or "teach" him or her. Only when a child did something really foolish—like breaking a soapstone lamp—might she or he be slapped.

Special times in a child's life, such as the loss of the first tooth or a boy's bringing home his first game, were noted with special rituals.

PLAY

Free play and organized games helped strengthen young bodies and develop physical dexterity, speed, hand-eye coordination, and accuracy. In their play they practiced the skills they would need as adults. For boys, this included hunting, fishing, and tool-making; for girls, cooking, sewing, and child care.

During racing and throwing contests the elders stressed that "winning"—beating someone else—was not the main point. They felt that everyone, as well as every *thing*, had a place in the order of life and that it was rude to make a point of one's excellence in some area.

Even pastimes that seemed just diversions (such as, Cat's Cradle, games of chance, guessing games) actually helped improve a child's ability to focus and strengthen small-muscle control.

TOYS

The toys of the three main cultures in this region were very similar: all had miniatures of adult tools, and of animals, boats, and people (dolls). All of these toys were used by the youngsters when they played at being grown up.

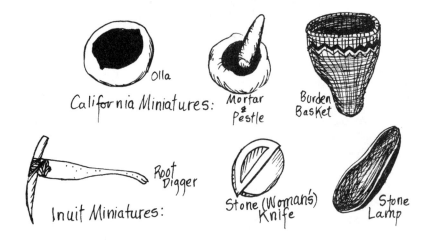

California Miniatures: Olla, Mortar & Pestle, Burden Basket

Inuit Miniatures: Root Digger, Stone (Woman's) Knife, Stone Lamp

GAMES

The children enjoyed games of tag, hide-and-seek, and variations on the hoop-and-spear game of California. In this game, a hoop was propelled across the ground while children tried to throw "a spear" through the moving ring. (See Photo 36.) In Alaska an animal

Photo 36. Mojave children play hoop-and-spear game, 1854. *Photo by B. Molhausen. Courtesy Museum of New Mexico.*

pelvis bone was used for throwing practice. In the Northwest, children tossed up into the air a fish tied to a stick and then tried "to spear" the fish on the other end of the stick.

Kids also had fun with balls, jump ropes, and guessing toys—including marked bones, gaming sticks, or dice.

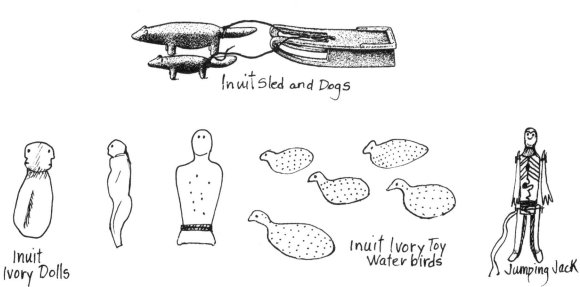

Inuit Sled and Dogs

Inuit Ivory Dolls

Inuit Ivory Toy Water birds

Jumping Jack

It is clear that early native Coastal children all loved activities that made them test and show their wit, strength, imagination, and luck.

COMING OF AGE

A very important time in a young person's life came around the age of 12 or 13, when initiation ceremonies marked their leaving childhood and entering adult life. During these ceremonies the young people were taught the ways of the tribe and given advice that would insure a long life, good health, many helpful offspring and, upon death, the rising of their spirit into the sky.

> Have respect for elders.
> Keep from anger.
> Be polite to family members.
>
> —Luiseño advice during initiation rites

Girls' Initiations

Many California tribes took note of a girl's coming of age with feasting, dancing, singing, and games. Friends and relatives came to celebrate and give the young girl many gifts. An older woman became her advisor and told her about her new duties (as a woman) and the special secrets of the universe.

In the Northwest, when a girl was about 12, she was shut away in a hut for a month to two years, depending on her rank. The first eight days were the hardest—she had to sit completely still with no food or water for four days; every day she was made to rub her face with a rough stone. If she broke these rules it was a disgrace for the tribe and her future was ruined.[2]

The rest of her time in the hut was spent practicing sewing and making baskets; she saw only older women relatives. In some tribes of the Northwest she had her family crest tattooed on her hand, or her lip was cut so she could wear a labret to show everyone that she now was a woman!

In northern Alaska a girl's face was tattooed to show that she was ready for marriage. An older woman, usually a relative, made the tattooed lines on the girl's chin by rubbing a thread and needle in lampblack and then pulling the thread through the girl's flesh. They were allowed to show their pain while it was being done. Even though it was painful, young girls looked forward to the time when they would be tattooed.

Boys' Initiations

In California the young boy of 12 or 13 often had to pass tests of courage before the tribe would see him as a grownup. An older man became the boy's lifelong advisor; he shared age-old secrets with the boy and instructed him in the history and lore of the tribe. During this time the boy might drink a special tea made of Angelica or Jimson Weed that would give him dreams or visions foretelling his future.

At about 12 a boy in the Northwest went to live with his mother's brother, who would be very strict with him. Every morning before dawn the uncle took the boy down to the freezing water and made him stay in it—up to his neck—until he was told to come out. Then the uncle lashed the boy all over with alder branches! These acts were meant to strengthen and cleanse the youngster so that he would have a good future.

He was taught to hunt, fish, and work wood. He was given daily jobs that were often very demanding and were for the good of the uncle's family. All this time the older man would teach the boy the ways of the clan.[3]

When a northern Alaska boy's voice changed, he got to wear a new style of short trousers. He would not have his lip cut for labrets until his father decided that the boy was ready to take on all the duties of being a man: to hunt and fish well and be ready for marriage. The boy carved his own small round lip plugs, *tuutoks*, which he put in as soon as the slits were cut on either side of his lower lip. (All during this private ceremony, the boy was *not* allowed to show any pain.)

Among groups that had guardian spirit quests, such rites took place when a boy was ten or twelve.

Notes for "Children and Play":

1. Hupa children in California were told the tale of the gaming dove, who, because he lacked self-control, brought pain and sadness to his whole family as well as to himself.

The Hupa Story of Xonsil'chwiw, the Dove

Dong'who'dun ("A long time ago...back in legendary times") Xonsil'chwiw lived with his wife and children in a village among his friends and relations. He was a good person, but he did have a weakness: he loved to gamble and once he got started he could hardly ever stop. When he couldn't find a Stick Game* in his own village, he'd move on to the next town to try'n find one.

The time came when he was goin' farther and farther from his home and family just lookin' for a game of chance.

Well, his wife was left all alone to try and take care of their children, but it was too much for her!

Came the time Xonsil'chwiw was many days' travel from home and he was gamblin' as ever when a relative came up and said, "You gotta come home, Xonsil'chwiw. Your wife is sick and your kids need you!"

Xonsil'chwiw looked up and said, "I'll be right there as soon as I finish this one last game!" So he played on and after a bit he started for home.

When he got back he looked for his house, but it was gone...burned down right to the earth, and all his family with it. Xonsil'chwiw began to moan and sob. He mourned his dead wife and all his dead children and he mourns to this day: "Hi'-yo-we-who'-who...hi'-yo-we-who'-who..."

No: n dik ("That's the end; there'll be no more talkin").

—Based on a Ray Baldy story in "The Creation of Language, a Yowlumni Story" by Matt Vera, in *News from Nature California*, vol. 7, no. 3, Summer 1993, page 29.

*See Lummi Stick Game in the *Activities* section.

2. Her failure to rub her face with a rock was seen as a sign that she would grow up to be a gossip and troublemaker. Breaking the fast showed that she would become a glutton or thief, or even a loose woman.

3. Some songs, tales, and dances were "owned" by the clan and could only be used by its members. The boy was taught the animals and supernatural creatures that went into his clan's art work—and the secret names of certain people, houses and even canoes!

Land rights were extremely important and involved fishing and hunting areas, as well as trade routes. They were the basis of future riches, and so also of rank for both the boy and his clan. The young man was expected to know these areas and routes and to protect them.

RELIGION AND BELIEFS

The lives of the early peoples centered around their spiritual beliefs. Every natural object had a spirit that was to be respected and honored. The Great Spirit was all powerful.

GOOD AND BAD SPIRITS

Throughout this region people believed that there were both good and bad spirits. Whenever bad things (illness, poor hunting, floods, droughts, earthquakes, accidents) happened, they believed that the balance in nature—the harmony between people and nature—had somehow been upset. (The early people of Alaska believed that thoughtless actions could upset the balance of the universe itself.) In times of trouble the leader of the group or the medicine person, the shaman[1] (*SHAH-muhn*), might call for a special ceremony to help bring Nature into balance again. These ceremonies might include prayers, the ritual use of tobacco,[2] fasting, dancing, and singing.

People in the Pacific Northwest believed that there were guardian spirits who could give you good luck and sometimes even supernatural powers! They also believed that there were monster spirits—ogres, evil dwarfs, huge man-eating birds, hideous sea monsters—who, although dangerous, might give you important gifts also.

When the Hazelnut Was a Guardian Spirit

Once a man was sittin' on a hillside crackin' hazelnuts. He was usin' a hammerstone when he hit one of the nuts just as usual, only *this* time the nut jumped up and flew off a little ways from him. He went over, got the nut and hit it again, but off it jumped, just like before!

"Well, okay," said the man, "I'll hand it to you—you've got spunk—but I'm gonna' crack your shell *any* way," and he grabbed the nut and held it tight. Then he hit it hard with his hammerstone. Once again that little ol' hazelnut just jumped up and *this* time it flew into the grass!

NOW the man was mad! He looked all over, but he could never find that nut.

Time passed, as it will, and one night a young boy on his vision quest came and sat down in the grass on that hillside. Suddenly a voice came to him in a dream!

"Hey, look at me, Son," said the spirit of the hazelnut, "and listen to what I have to say. Nobody can hold me *or* hurt me—even if I'm hit right on the head! When I hide, nobody ever finds me. Because I'm strong, I will give you strength. And if you always do as I say, you will have my powers. No enemy will ever hold you. You'll be able to jump away and hide right before their eyes AND they'll never be able to find you if you just do as I say."

The boy woke from his dream and went back to his village. He never told *any* one about that hazelnut. From then on he always listened to its advice. When he grew up he found that he had a strange power: he could get away from anybody who tried to capture him. Even when he was caught and held prisoner, he was always able to get away in the end. He grew to be a great warrior among the Yakima people and it was all through the help of his guardian spirit, the little hazelnut!

The Yupik people of Alaska believed in two worlds that were both going on at once: the world that was seen and the invisible world of the spirits. During important times such as birth, coming of age, and death, it was especially important to follow the religious rules—or else bad spirits, *tunghat*,[3] would cross over to the visible world and harm people!

CEREMONIAL BUILDINGS

Some coastal groups had a special place in which they held their religious ceremonies, such as the California earth lodge and the Eskimo kashim. (See **Shelter**.) In the Northwest during mid-winter certain areas of the longhouse were changed into sacred spaces while religious festivals were being held.

Sweat Baths

The people of this region used sweat baths to clean their bodies, to help heal illnesses, and as a religious act. During a sweat, a prayer was given to the Great Spirit asking for purity, strength, and good fortune in whatever work was soon to be done.[4]

Frame of sweatbath

CEREMONIES AND RITUALS

Ceremonies marked special times in people's lives including birth, naming of children, coming of age (see **Children and Play**), marriage, and death. They also marked important times—such as the change of seasons—in the life of the community as a whole.

The early people held a sacred ceremony—with its singing, dancing and praying—in order to keep promises to honor the Great Spirit and to stay in close touch with Nature and its many spirits.

World Renewal Ceremony

The Hupa, Karok, and Yurok in Northern California held an annual ceremony every fall during which the shamans carried out secret rites for the renewal of nature.

The men of the tribe displayed (on poles or on their bodies) the heads and hides of white deer and carried obsidian blades. They performed a slow plaintive ritual dance to show their gratitude for the blessings of the past and to ask for good fortune in the coming season.

Becoming a Shaman

There was a ritual in the Northwest by which young men tried to find and overpower their supernatural spirit. If they were successful, they might receive special healing powers.

There was no guarantee that a man would be successful in meeting his special spirit, but each man had to keep trying. What follows are excerpts from a first-person account of a Coast Salish man describing his six-year struggle of winter fasting and hardship until he was, at last, given healing powers.

"So from spring to autumn I fished and hunted and played with the other boys of the village. But when winter came again I resumed my fasting: I roamed the woods, bathed in its icy pools, rubbed myself with the boughs of evergreen trees, ate nothing, but drank water copiously and gave it up again. After each bath I prayed to Him Who Dwells Above, and I danced until I fell to the ground exhausted, then at night I slept on beds of branches or in the hollow of some tree. Gradually my skin became hard like the bark of trees, with which I scrubbed it. No cold could penetrate it; the rain and the snow that fell on me seemed warm.

"Each time that I went out my sufferings seemed a little less, until after the first hour of waking I felt light and vigorous, and was conscious of neither hunger nor thirst."

(**After spending six winters this way, between the ages of 9 and 15, this Salish boy at last received his healing powers.**)

". . . (One day) I reached the place where the medicine man was singing, a house unlike any that I had ever seen before. He who was behind me whispered: 'Go inside. This is he for whom you are seeking, the true medicine man for whom you have undergone penance all these years.'

"I entered. The medicine man was kneeling on the floor, and beside him was his water, in some mystical vessel that was neither a dish nor a basket. He turned and looked at me. 'Poor boy,' he said. 'So you have come at last. Kneel down beside me.'

"I knelt beside him. In front of us appeared every sickness that afflicts mankind, concentrated in a single human being. 'Wash your hands and wrists in this water.' I washed them. 'Now lay your hands on that sickness and remove it.'

"I laid my hands on the patient and cupped his sickness out with them. He rose to his feet, cured. 'That is how you shall remove every sickness. You shall chant the song you have heard me sing and cup out the sickness with your hands. Now go.'"

—Old Pierre of Katzie, c. 1895,
The Faith of a Salish Indian by Diamond Jennes, pg.63,
(The British Columbia Museum, 1955)

The Bladder Ceremony[5]

In Alaska in early December the Inuit celebrated the Bladder Festival in the kashim. Women brought food to the participating men, the one time during the year women were allowed to enter the ceremonial house.

The Bladder Festival was a four-day ceremony held at the end of the hunting season to honor the *inua*, the souls of the sea animals that had been killed during the previous year. The bladder of each slain sea animal was dried and saved for this occasion as, according to Inuit tradition, it held the animal's soul.

In preparation for the ceremony the kashim was thoroughly cleaned. The bladders were blown up and painted with designs and then hung from the walls and ceiling. Among these inflated bladders hung large carved animal puppets whose eyes, mouths, wings, and hands could be controlled by pulling on dangling strings.

A fire was always blazing and the people were warned not to make loud noises which could frighten the *inuas* in the hanging bladders. The points of harpoons and spears were taken off their shafts to calm the animal spirits' fears. Songs and dances were given, using the calls and movements of sea birds and animals. Funny speeches were given to them and food was offered to the spirits.

On the fourth night the shaman climbed to the roof of the kashim and gave a speech. The bladders were taken down and the hunters followed the shaman to the sea, to a large hole in the ice. There the hunters tore open the bladders and thrust them into the water. As they did this they listened carefully to the sinking bladders, hoping to hear the *inuas* say: "We are happy with you for giving us such a fine festival and so your next hunting season will be filled with success!"

Inuit Masks

Masks

Masks were a spectacular part of religious rites because they replaced the human face with an inhuman or supernatural one. Among the northern Eskimo, simple wooden masks of the human face were buried with their owners.

Haida Mask

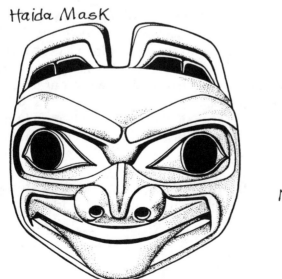

Northern Eskimo Mask

DEATH

The Native Americans saw death not as a puzzle or as an end to things but as one of the parts of the cycle of nature, a stage that all living creatures must finally pass through.

The Lower Colorado River peoples of southeastern California cremated their dead. A specially built death arbor, *keruk*, was used once a year for a memorial service in which they mourned and remembered all those who had gone that year. Lifesize tule sculptures were made to represent the deceased; these were dressed and baskets of food were placed in the net bags on their backs.

To begin the memorial ceremony, the people retold the story of how the first death house was built by their Creator. For one week the people sang, danced, prayed, cried, and feasted. Finally the tule sculptures were burned, along with the keruk, so that the souls of the dead could go on with their long journey to the Land of the Great Spirit.

Many southern Coastal tribes buried their dead in cemeteries near their villages. Personal items such as baskets, tools, and clothing were often buried with them.

In northern California men and women showed their love and respect for the dead person by cutting off or singeing their own hair, close to the head. Another way to show mourning was to rub tar into one's hair, or to cover one's face with charcoal and ground-up clam shells.

Some groups in the Northwest believed that the spirits of the dead stayed near the body at the place of death and that such ghosts were dangerous to the living. Therefore, the body was quickly taken away from the village to its last resting place, which could be (depending on where in the Northwest one lived) a storage box, a grave house (Haida), a tall tree, a memorial pole or platform, or a canoe that would then be burned.

The people in this area had no particular belief in a heaven or hell.

The inland peoples of Alaska weren't afraid to die because they believed that each person's spirit would be born again in a new child—just as the spirits of slain creatures would be reborn in new animals.

"Let (the white man) be just and kindly with my people, for the dead are not powerless. Dead, did I say? There is no death, only a change of worlds."

—Chief Seathl, 1854

Religion gave the early people a sense of community and a feeling that they had some power over their destiny. Religion gave their lives order and meaning.

Notes for "Religion and Beliefs":

1. *The Shaman* was the medicine person, the seer, or the holy one. There were several different kinds:

    *   *The Healing Doctor* was called when there was a serious illness. The Shaman sang, danced, and used personal power to drive out the evil spirit causing the sickness. Sometimes such doctors would suck on the patient's body to pull out the evil. A shaman was paid in money and gifts, but was expected to return the payment if the patient did not recover.

    *   *The Bear Doctor* had the power to turn himself into a bear and destroy the enemies of his people.

    "Among the first created people of the Bear tribe, some of the head men could and did change themselves into bears and lived with them and slept like they do through the winter. But not any more can these things be done."

    —Francisco Patencio, Cahuilla, 1943

    *   *The Rain (or Weather) Doctor* was common in southern California; it was believed he could bring rain and stop floods.

    *   *The Rattlesnake Doctor* knew how to prevent and how to cure snake bites. Rattlesnake dances were held by the Central California tribes.

2. Tobacco was widely used in California for ceremonial purposes. The shaman would use it to clear the air of any evil forces. He did this by blowing smoke in each of the sacred directions. Ritual tobacco was smoked by both men and women during such events.

Tobacco was harvested from wild plants; among the Tubatulabal of central California the women prepared it by drying it in the sun, sprinkling it with water, redrying it, and then pounding the leaves into a powder. Such tobacco was smoked in cane pipes in the Central Valley; in other areas, people used whatever materials were locally available to make pipes: oak, elderberry, maple root, etc.

3. Inuits in general were concerned about ghosts, dead souls, and good and evil spirits; they thought that violating ceremonial rules (taboos) could bring death. Shamans were expected to protect the Inuit against these supernatural powers that humans were incapable of understanding.

4. During a sweat bath the Inuit breathed through a woven-grass mouthpiece to keep the smoke out of his lungs. Once sweat-soaked, he washed himself with urine, which acted like a soap to remove body oils. Then he went outside and bathed in clear water.

5. *The Inuit Ceremonial Cycle* was prepared each year by the group's shamans and elders. This included:
   - *The Asking Festival* (Petuqtaq), an event held between villages to cement kin ties through the exchange of requested gifts.
   - *The Feast of the Dead* (Merr'aq) made sure that those who had died would have plenty of food, drink, and clothing in the after-life.
   - *The Bladder Festival* (Nakaciua) is described in the main text.
   - *The Inviting-in Feast* (Kekek/Itrukalar), last festival of the year, was held when food was getting scarce. The spirits were invited to come and share in what little the people had left. The people thanked the spirits for their help in the past and said how they hoped that the spirits would again assist them during the upcoming hunting season.

SOCIAL GROUPS AND GOVERNMENT

The native people saw themselves as members of their family first and foremost. In some groups there were over fifty words to describe different kinds of relatives. Throughout this region a person without a family was considered worthless.

CALIFORNIA

Most of the peoples of California lived in and around villages. A group of neighboring villages, usually less than twelve, might make up a band that was headed by a single chief or a council; a band was like a small tribe.

Bands belonging to the same big tribal group might live far away from one another and not even speak the same language.[1] They might visit one another to trade and take part in shared ceremonies, which showed they had old connections; but, for the most part, each band governed itself.

The early California people followed clear social rules that showed them how to lead their lives. Each person had to be helpful to the others—and this brought about cooperation, sharing, patience, and a sense of responsibility. Many of their customs were based on tribal religion, which also added to their sense of community.

Leaders

Either men or women could be community leaders. Often leadership roles were passed from father to son or mother to daughter. Leaders had to prove themselves worthy of their jobs by being dignified, wise, and brave.

The chiefs or captains, as they were called, usually had a group of wise older helpers—a council—to give them advice.[2] The shamans were also called in to help.

A chief had to direct ceremonies, settle arguments between families, plan trading trips, see that food was shared fairly, and encourage people to work hard and help one another.

War

Most native Californians lived peacefully because there were good sources of food and plenty of land; wars were few and were fought as a reluctant last resort.

There *were* rivalries and feuds, however, and some groups acted aggressively. In the north the Modoc and Ukiah went on raiding parties against their enemies. The Kurok, armed with bows and arrows, went into battle wearing complete upper-torso armor of thick basketry! In the south the Mojave had many wars with the Halchidhomas and with tribes from Arizona.

Even peaceful groups were somewhat suspicious of one another when it came to boundaries and trading. A group that felt it had been wronged might refuse for years to trade something that their rivals needed badly, such as salt. Feuds in northern California were sometimes ended by having a Settlement Dance.

The Settlement Dance

The men taking part stood in two long rows, each facing their enemies. Each dancer was armed and his face was painted black. Baskets by the fire held the goods and money that would be used to pay back each side to make up their differences. The baskets were sung over and then for a long time the men danced side to side. At last the payments were made and the argument was ended.

OREGON AND WASHINGTON

Because their food and building materials were so easy to find, these early people had free time. They used it to come up with a rich way of governing and living together.

Kinship Groups

Family ties were important to these people, who got power and protection through their many relations. Each kin-group usually governed itself and gave out its own terms of justice. Kinship ties kept the peace among groups; such ties were strengthened by intermarriage, by trading, and by sharing ceremonies—especially potlatches!

Your standing in the village was handed down to you. Each line of ancestors (clan) had special rights: the right to hunt and fish in a certain place, the right to do certain dances, the right to leadership, and the right to use certain crests.

Crests

Every clan took an animal or mythical creature for its particular representative or crest. These "protectors" were believed to help those who were of their crest. Individual men could also have private crests that were earned by undergoing hardships, torture, or fasting.

Some commonly used animal crest figures were: Killer Whale, Bear, Wolf, Beaver, Raven, Eagle, Hawk, Frog, Owl, and even Mosquito.

Mythical creatures used as crests included: Thunderbird, Sisiutl (a two-headed serpent), Sun, and Moon.

Totem[3] Poles or Crest Monuments

Totem poles were wooden monuments that declared the crests and ancestry of important families. They were made and used by the Salish, Quinault, Makah, Haida, and Tlingit, among others.[4]

In a culture with no written language, the pole carvings were meant to be reminders of historic events, important people, and family legends. Crest poles were not made to be worshipped nor to be part of religious ceremonies.

There were several different types of poles, each with a different purpose. They included memorial poles, mortuary poles, potlatch poles, heraldic poles, house pillars, and ridicule poles.[5]

Rank and Wealth

Most villages had three classes of people: the highest ranked (chiefs and nobles), the commoners, and the slaves (who had been purchased or captured in war[6].) The nobles and chiefs did not mistreat the commoners, as happens in some cultures, because they were relatives, and so were to be treated with respect.

Chilkat blanket or robe

Crest animal is an eagle.

The most important wealth—land, lodges, coppers[7]—was owned by kin-groups rather than by individuals. In these communities wealth and high standing went together. Your personal riches (sea otter and marmot skins, Chilkat blankets,[8] dentalium shells, canoes, slaves) were all signs of your power and how well you were doing.

Potlatch

The potlatch was an important part of native life from Oregon to Alaska. This elaborate festival was marked by the host's giving away incredible amounts of food and expensive objects. The more he gave, the more honored and respected he was by his guests and the others in his tribe. The gift-giving took up several days as did the feasting, dancing, singing, and tests of physical strength. Gambling and storytelling continued long into the nights.[9]

War

A kin-group would go to war to retaliate for crimes committed against one of their own by those of another group.[10] The aggrieved group had to strike back or otherwise it would be thought weak and contemptible. Northwest coast people also raided to get "rank," taking the honor and riches of their neighbors by force.

A war chief dressed in fancy armor would lead the raiding party, which was armed with clubs and daggers. Surprise and deception were the most favored tactics.[11]

ALASKA

The Haida and the Tlingit

The Haida and the Tlingit behaved in many ways like the other Northwest people described earlier: kinship ties and wealth were important to them, families owned crests, and potlatches were given to show rank.

The Haida were well known for the beautiful costumes, masks, headdresses, and musical instruments they used during their ceremonies.

Both the Haida and the Tlingit lived in separate groups of villages that were independent from one another. Family groups were related through the mother's side (matrilineal) and their big plank houses were passed on through these female lines of relationship.

The Tlingits divided themselves into two large groups (known as moieties): the Raven and the Wolf.[12] A person belonged to his or her mother's moiety and had to marry outside it, usually with a person of the father's side. A moiety was divided into several clans, each with its own leader; the Raven moiety had some 27 clans.

Each clan had land rights and owned several crests that important members showed on their many personal objects, and on totem poles placed in front of their ancestral houses.

Eskimo

Eskimo men were judged by their hunting skills, bravery, endurance, modesty, and their treatment of older people. It was also important that a man be willing to share his game or possessions with others.

Inuit women were judged by their sewing and food preparation skills, courage, stamina, modesty, respect for elders, and their ability to have children.

An Inuit village had no judges or courts. Community taboos (acts forbidden by tradition) and the wish to be respected by his family and friends "told" the Inuit how to behave. Group approval was the highest reward—just as being laughed at, or shunned, was the most awful punishment.

A person who was continually making trouble or who committed a very serious crime—such as murder or wife stealing[13]—might, by group agreement, be put to death. The criminal was stabbed or strangled to death by a close relative so as to avoid setting up a feud between two families.

Although there were no official laws, a man who felt wronged could challenge his enemy to a formal fist fight in front of the community. Only one blow could be struck at a time; the challenged man went first and the two men alternated blows from then on until someone gave up or was knocked out. This settled the matter. Disputes could also be worked out by ear-pulling, nose-pulling, and mouth-stretching contests.

Then there was the Song Battle, held in the ceremonial house in front of an adult audience. Two men, or women, who were angry with each other would take turns singing insulting verses about his or her enemy. Whichever person got more laughs from the crowd was considered the winner!

War

The Arctic Inuit tried to work out their feuds when they met each other at fishing and hunting grounds, or at the big yearly trading fairs. Seldom did one village or group raid another.

Slave raids were a problem for the Aleuts. Aleut houses had their entry holes on the roof, so a surprise attack could trap everyone inside. The Aleuts dealt with this in three ways:

1. Lookouts were posted to watch for approaching enemies.
2. The house walls had secret spaces where people could hide until the enemy retreated.
3. The house also had tunnels that led to the beach and the family's canoes.

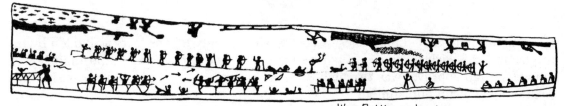

War Battles on Land and Sea

Notes for "Social Groups and Government":

1. Bands in a tribal group *were* related by language; but over thousands of years groups that had a common language at first, separated into local bands or triblets and their languages drifted apart.

2. When a new leader was needed, he or she was often chosen from this council.

3. The word *totem* is from Algonquin (the Cree word is *ototema*: his relations) and means an animal or natural object thought to be related by blood to a specific family or clan, and taken as its symbol.

4. The Coast Salish did not put up the traditional heraldic poles. They carved their house posts and made welcoming figures, 10 to 12 feet tall, with raised arms held in place by pegs. They also made mortuary figures.

   The Canadian Nootka, Kwakiutl, Bella Coola, Bella Bella, and Tsimshian all made pole monuments.

5. • *Memorial poles* were used to honor an important person at the time of his death. Many of these poles are plain with the crest figure of the person's clan at the top of the bare pole.

Memorial Pole

— Haida Mortuary Poles with stones holding down lids —

• *Mortuary poles*

   ... and a battered row of totem poles circled the bay. Many of them were mortuary poles, high with square fronts on top. The fronts were carved with totem designs of birds and beasts. The tops of the poles behind these carved fronts were hollowed out and the coffins stood each in its hole, on its end, the square front hiding it. Some of the old mortuary poles were broken and you saw skulls peeping out through the cracks.

—Emily Carr, *Klee Wyck*, 1885

- *A Potlatch pole* was raised when a potlatch was given. It celebrated and marked this important social occasion. (See "Potlatch" in this section.)

- *Heraldic poles* announced the social standing of a wealthy man or head of a house. It carried the family's crest and was attached to the front of the building; often it had an oval hole (doorway) through which you passed to enter the house.

- *House pillars*: In early Northwest houses the inside posts that held up the ceiling of a building were often decorated with the owner's crests. Because they have been protected from the weather, they are often found in excellent condition.

- *Ridicule or Shame poles* were erected to embarrass or shame an individual or family for its failure to pay a debt *or* for breaking a trust. The poles were taken down when the wrong was corrected.

Ridicule (or Amusing) Totem Pole Figure

6. Most were women or children who couldn't defend themselves during a raid. Although they usually lived in the owner's house, they were thought of as less than human. They could be sold or traded and were treated either well or badly at the whim of the owner. Once in a while a slave's family was able to pay a large ransom to have the slave returned.

    Although slaves were used to do work, they were owned mainly as a sign of honor and wealth. To have slaves proved that you were either good in battle or very rich. Often slaves were killed to show the owner's disregard for riches. For example, as a new house was finished, a slave might be thrown into each of the post holes into which the huge carved door posts were then sunk.

7. Coppers were important objects, especially in the potlatch. (See below.) Copper was collected in stream beds, melted down, and beaten into plaques about one and a half to three feet long. (See Photo 37.)

    Here there is a mystery; these plaques were traded from the Copper River area, but it is thought that the people who lived there did not have the skills to produce this quality of metal work. It is possible that this is a case of early archaeology, i.e., the people who traded these coppers dug them out from a stash left by some earlier people.

    These pieces were traded southward from the Copper River. Many were decorated along the way with shallow engravings by artists of the north coastlands. As they continued to be traded southward, they became more and more costly.

Photo 37. Haida man with copper stands in front of 6-beamed Haida house, prior to 1906. *Courtesy British Columbia Provincial Museum, Victoria.*

Coppers were sometimes broken up during a memorial potlatch and the pieces ("bones of the dead") were given to important guests. Later, coppers became a part of marriage payments.

8. These regal dancing blankets of green, yellow, black, and white were worn on important (ceremonial) occasions. They were made of mountain goat wool, yellow cedar bark, and natural dyes. The Chilkat blanket or robe was named after the Tlingit tribe whose weavers specialized in its making. Women wove these robes from blueprints (patterns) painted on thin cedar boards by the men.

9. Potlatch means "to give away" in the Chinook trade slang. This complicated festival was important because it was used to announce and celebrate major changes in the standing of a kin-group or one of its members. Leadership, titles, crests, and names were displayed and transferred in front of the many guests, who acted as witnesses and were expected to keep the memory of this potlatch alive through stories that became a kind of legal record in a language that had no writing.

It could take up to ten years for a family to put together a potlatch; this, as well as the gift-giving, spread wealth from the rich to the rest of the community. The host might be "penniless" after paying for all the gifts, foods, expensive costumes—as well as the dancers, the singers, and the storytellers—but his wealth measured in honor and respect (and envy?) would be much greater than before. And his guests would remember his potlatch forever!

Here is a legend of the Quillayute, explaining how the potlatch originated.

How We Got the Potlatch

Long ago all the birds in the world were of the same gray color—the robin, the finch, the eagle, the hummingbird, all were gray. Then one day a strange bird came and sat in the ocean in front of a Quillayute village. All the young men ran down to the beach and tried to kill it, but nobody was able to hit it. Every day, Jaybird, a slave of Eagle, watched the hunters trying to shoot the strange bird.

Then one day Eagle said to Jaybird, "Hey, you know what? I bet my children could get that odd looking bird!" "You're kidding," said Jaybird. "The young men of our village haven't been able to get that bird! What makes you think that your GIRLS could do it?"

Now Eagle's daughters overheard this talk and they went into the woods and stayed there all day though they were girls—get this: they were making arrows!

Well, time passed. The young men still had not been able to get that strange bird.

Then one morning before dawn the two girls came into the village with their hair tied so that it hung down in their faces. No one knew who they were so they got into a canoe and paddled out to where the strange bird was. The older sister stood up, took her bow, and shot three arrows. The third arrow brought down the odd bird.

"We did it! Now let's use those colorful feathers for presents!" So they returned to shore and said to the amazed villagers: "Tell Jaybird to call all of the birds together and have them meet us tomorrow at our lodge!"

The next morning all the birds in the world were there. The Eagle went up front and he said:

"My girls did it. They got that strange bird and now they want to give each of you a gift."

The sisters took the colored feathers and gave certain colors to each bird: brown and rust to the robin, yellow and black to the chickadee, shades of blue to the bluebird. The girls gave and gave out the feathers until they were all gone.

Ever since then, each bird has had certain colors. And ever since that day there have been potlatches where you give and give 'til there's nothing left. This story is, in fact, the story of the first potlatch ever held!

10. First they would ask for repayment or, in the case of a murder, the death of a person of equal rank. Blood-payments sometimes satisfied this demand.

11. The fake peace treaty was a favorite trick. When the enemy was weakened, some captives were sent back to them, bringing with them gifts and an offer of peace; if the other side accepted, a peace feast was arranged. Then each warrior was assigned a victim and, at a signal, each of the visitors to the "peace feast" was killed or taken into slavery.

12. In some very large villages, there was a third moiety, the Eagle.

13. Eskimo wife-loaning was not done lightly. It was usually an agreement between families that wanted closer kinship ties.

THE EUROPEANS COME

The native people of all the Pacific Coast state areas had their lives and their cultures changed forever by the coming of the Europeans. The dates of contact varied but similar consequences resulted everywhere.

The Europeans claimed the land for their respective sovereigns, who wanted the natural resources of this New World: safe harbors, baleen and oil from whales, fur pelts, free labor—and gold, if there was any to be had. Often these white men also wanted to save the souls of the natives and turn these "primitives" into civilized beings.

The first European settlements in California and Alaska took place in the mid-1700s, but there had been contact long before that. In 1542 Spanish galleons under the command of Captains Cabrillo and Ferrelo cruised up the coasts of California and Oregon looking for a harbor where they could refit and resupply their ships. In 1579 the Englishman Francis Drake spent five weeks anchored north of San Francisco Bay, repairing his ship. He met with the Miwoks and reported to his queen of the rich land and pleasant people.

The first Europeans to set foot on Alaskan soil were members of a Russian expedition that came ashore at Kayak Island in 1741. In the 1750s Russian fur traders regularly kidnapped Aleut women and children every year, forcing Aleut men to provide huge quantities of sea otter pelts before returning their families to them.

In the early 1760s the eastern Aleuts tried to resist the Russians, but it was not possible to win against their guns. While under Russian rule the Aleuts took on—or were made to accept—an odd mixture of new ways. They learned to speak Russian, began wearing Russian clothes, and little by little gave up their sod shelters for Russian wooden frame houses. Many took Russian names and thousands joined the Russian Orthodox Church.

In 1799 the Russians set up a fort at Old Sitka in southwest Alaska. The Tlingits immediately opposed their presence, and, in 1802, drove out the Russians, who returned two years later to set up another post at New Sitka. The Tlingits continued their resistance for 65 years, until the United States bought Alaska.

It wasn't until the middle of the 18th century, when it looked as if Russia or England might try to take California (and so threaten Mexico to the south!), that Spain moved to settle California. In 1769 Governor Portola (of Baja California) and Father Junipero Serra began setting up a chain of Catholic mission/school/forts along the southern and central California coast; eventually, 21 missions were established. Even though some Native California groups resisted being worked by the soldiers, they were not able to organize against the Spanish and, in the end, the native people were practically enslaved.[1]

The years between 1750 and 1850 were a time of great change in the West of North America. Expeditions and exploration brought Native Americans more and more in touch with Europeans. At first frontier trade was good for both the whites and the Pacific coast peoples, but these Russian, French, Spanish, and English traders brought more than cloth, beads, and cast iron pots; they also brought diseases and alcohol, which killed large numbers of the indigenous people, sometimes wiping out whole tribes.[2]

The completion of the California and Oregon Trails (mid 1850s) and, later, the arrival of the railroads in Seattle, San Francisco, and Los Angeles (1883-1884) encouraged more and more people "to come out West" and settle.

Each time gold was discovered in California and Alaska, treasure hunters overran the land. Native areas were divided and built on and the wildlife and grazing grounds were destroyed.

The Pacific Coastal peoples all experienced some loss of their homelands. In the Northwest, Indian lands were settled on by European-Americans with no treaties and no land reserves being set aside for the natives.[3] It was the same in southwest Alaska. (See Photo 38.)

Photo 38. Tsimshian Mortuary Houses show European influence. *Courtesy Vancouver Public Library.*

In 1846 Oregon Country (Oregon and Washington) became part of the United States as a settlement with Britain. Then in 1850 California became an American state. In 1867 the United States bought Alaska from Russia for $7.2 million.[4]

On the whole the United States government had a general policy of relocation of indigenous peoples to smaller, less desirable lands. Too often the treaties they signed with the natives were ignored or broken when these agreements did not favor American commercial interests.

For 30 years groups of Pacific Coastal Native Americans would protest—often with violence—the forced treaties and land takeovers (allowed) by the United States government.[5]

Starting in the 1870s industrialists came and set up canneries and mining operations in Washington and Alaska. Indians became low-paid laborers and left their villages to live in canning and mining housing.[6]

During the second half of the 19th century and well into the 20th century, the European-Americans tried to convince the Indians to stop holding their ceremonies, even outlawing them in some places.[7] Native children were taken from their families and forced to go to far-off federal schools where they were not allowed to speak their own languages. Little by little the native cultures were broken down.[8] (See Photo 39.)

Photo 39. Potlatch with piles of gifts. *Courtesy Vancouver Public Library.*

In 1914 the United States entered World War I. Native Americans from all of the Pacific coast states enlisted and fought for their country before they were even allowed to vote. Citizenship was granted in 1924 to all Native Americans born in the United States.

Following World War II, in which 25,000 Native Americans served, the United States government helped thousands of Indians relocate to San Francisco and Los Angeles, where their chances for employment were better than on isolated reservations.

In 1959 Alaska became a state.

With each year there was increasing political involvement in the Pacific coast states among the Native American youth, in particular. Organizations such as The Alaskan Federation of Natives, the American Indian Movement, and The National Indian Youth Council were formed. Political actions on behalf of environmental concerns—fishing rights, contamination of rivers, overlogging of forests, strip mining—were demonstrated.

Some progress was made. Lands were returned to Native Alaskans, Haida, Tlingit and Yakimas; bills were passed to protect American Indian resources and to provide for Native American subsistence hunting and fishing. Other legislation protected Native American gravesites and assured the return to the tribes of Indian remains and burial objects.

And yet even through all these hardships and disruptions, the Pacific coast peoples kept their sense of who they were and who their ancestors had been.

Notes for "The Europeans Come":

1. The Mission period was a disaster for Native Californians. Though it lasted just 60-some years, this was time enough to nearly destroy them. Their food, clothing, housing and working patterns, religion, and languages were all changed. It ended in 1821 when Mexico won its War of Independence against Spain—and California became a Mexican holding. Many of the priests returned to Spain and the missions were sold or stood empty. Fifteen thousand Mission Indians were left with nowhere to go; many became wandering and homeless.

   During the years of Spanish rule 81,000 California Indians were made to work for the padres. During this time more than 60,000 of these native people died or were killed.

2. These epidemics, which started in 1782, continued for a hundred years. They included outbreaks of smallpox (Sanpoils, Washington, 1782-1783); malaria, diphtheria, influenza (California and Oregon, 1830s); and measles (Cayuse, at the Presbyterian Mission School, Oregon, 1847) that devastated people who had no immunity to these Old World diseases. In some places where there was heavy contact with Europeans, up to 90% of the Inuit and Chinooks died in the epidemics.

3. One exception: a group of Tsimshian Indians with the missionary William Duncan were given a reserve.

4. The new United States laws did not allow Native Americans to own guns, to testify in court, or to vote in elections.

5. Among the resisting groups were the Yuma and Mojave of California; the Walla Walla, Umatilla, and Cayuse of Oregon; and the Coeur d'Alene Paiutes, Spokane, and Nez Perce of Washington.

6. Starting in the 1870s the museums of North America and Europe became interested in collecting Northwest art because they believed this culture would soon disappear. They sent collectors to buy all the old ceremonial pieces and many of the totem poles; these collectors, without permission, also stripped the graveyards of their carvings.

7. In the Northwest, where the Europeans wanted to be able to trade in peace, they would not allow the tribes to war with one another. As a consequence, the potlatch—which *had* been a statement of group respect and loyalty—*now* became a way to let out frustration and to insult and shame your rivals. With time, and the presence of mass-produced goods, the potlatch became incredibly elaborate and overrich. This made the Christian missionaries in the Northwest uncomfortable. They saw potlatches as being wasteful and uncivilized. In 1884 the Canadian government outlawed potlatches. For 50 years whites tried to control this ceremony,

but it just went underground, forcing the Haida and Tlingit to have their ceremonies in secret.

8. The rifle also contributed to the breakdown of traditional life in the north. It allowed the native hunter to kill caribou, seal, and walrus in large numbers. In just a few years the Inuit killed so much game that the animal population in the Arctic fell drastically.

Hunting with rifles meant that there was no longer any reason to make harpoons, clubs, spears, or even kayaks. The hunter no longer "needed" his friends to go on a hunt or make a kill. The ideas of cooperation and community were quickly weakened.

Lone hunter with rifle

THE COASTAL INDIANS TODAY

We have seen in the previous chapter how destructive the European diseases were to the indigenous peoples—even threatening them with extinction. But the Native Americans continued to struggle for life and they survived; in the last fifty years their populations have been steadily increasing.[1]

What of the lives of these First Americans today? How do they fare in the contemporary United States?

The statistics can seem bleak: less than 10% of American Indians still speak their native language, their unemployment rate is 45%, the average Native American worker earns less than $7,000 a year, and 45% of all native people live below the poverty level.

The Native American who lives in a city is often disconnected from other people there. Alcohol is a serious problem in urban settings as well as on the reservations.

Native American teenagers often feel as if they don't "belong," that the future is without promise: half finish high school, only 4% complete college, and the rate of teenage suicide attempts (one in six has tried suicide) is four times higher than that of other teenagers in the United States.

These figures are sobering, but they do not tell the entire story. In each of the Pacific Coast states native people are working hard to change such statistics by recapturing old traditions and starting new business enterprises.

Recently the development of gambling casinos on reservation lands has become a political issue in these states, as well as in the rest of the United States. Oregon and Washington have 17 of these American Indian-run casinos (as many as there are in California, which has twice as many Native Americans living there). Although the gaming business seems like a quick road to riches for the native peoples, it brings up both economic and political concerns and questions.[2]

"The issue of Indian sovereignty hangs in the balance as Indians cautiously negotiate the maze of overlapping state and federal jurisdictions and control."

—George Russell, Saginaw-Chippewa, *The American Indian Digest,* page 54

Today many Coastal native people are teaching their children the legends, traditions, and history of their ancestors.[3]

Families are sharing the old dances, songs, and ceremonies with friends and relatives. During the Gatherings or ceremonies, the children wear the dance regalia, sing the songs, and continue the ancient ways. (See Photo 40.)

Photo 40. Ceremony of thanksgiving in mat house. *Photo by D. Spuler. Courtesy Bancroft Library, University of California at Berkeley.*

The young ones join their elders in prayers for peace and balance in the world, helping to renew the world much as their ancestors did centuries ago.

The native languages are slowly being relearned.[4] Negotiations with museums are succeeding in getting ritual art objects and sacred remains returned to their appropriate tribes. The Native Americans are forming environmental groups and working for environmental change.

BASKETMAKER ACTIVISTS

Native California basketmakers have protested about timber companies spraying the forests with herbicides that kill basketry plants and endanger the health of their small rural communities. Fifteen years ago, after reports of unusually high rates of cancer, birth defects, and miscarriages began to surface, the Hupa tribe banned herbicide spraying on its forest lands. Currently the Karuk tribe is working with the Trees Foundation and the U.S. Forest Service to develop an Ecosystem Management Strategy for the Bluff Creek watershed.

On January 25, 1993, Jennifer Bates (North Mewuk), Chair of the California Indian Basketweavers Association, sent a letter to the California Department of Pesticide Regulation:

> "We assert that it is our right to practice basketweaving in the tradition that has been handed down to us and that we are passing on to our children. It is our right to do so without being poisoned by pesticides....
>
> "Both hand and mouth contact are made with many plant materials by basketweavers. Weavers have suffered the loss of teeth and numbness of the mouth after processing materials which have been sprayed. What other illness or deaths may have been caused by such contact cannot be known. If a plant is dying or dead as a result of spraying, it will not be harvested. But how is a weaver to know if a plant has been recently sprayed?"[5]

The Department of Pesticide Regulation has begun pesticide residue sampling in central California. The hoped-for result is the "elimination of potentially harmful effects to Native American health" from the use of roadside sprays.

> "I think our culture will come back, but not as it was before. It'll be remembered. It will. People are going to wish—Why didn't we leave it like it was? Why didn't we leave all this [natural world] alone instead of destroying the vegetation to put in these shopping centers, which we can't even afford half the things that they sell?"
>
> —Juanita Centeno, Mission Chumash teacher of Chumash crafts and lore

Besides basketmaking, other crafts—including woodcarving, jewelry and doll-making—are being reestablished today. For example, the Pomo women are again making their redwood bark dolls that demonstrate the people's inventiveness and resilience.

> "I think what it [doll-making] did for me was to develop a sense of patience. Because you have to have patience to make toys.
>
> "...A lot of people probably think that the Poman people are no longer in existence. We are, like the redwood tree. ...Nobody wiped us out, ...we're growin' in number. And we're here. Our people are still here. ..."
>
> —Otis Parrish, Kashaya Pomo

THE SALMON PEOPLE

The salmon and the people of the Northwest have always been as one. Through centuries the salmon has provided nutrition for the people and inspired sacred ceremonies, sacred sites, and creation stories. As they say, "The people are the salmon." Over the last six decades the link between the people and the salmon has been almost completely destroyed.

Once 100,000,000 salmon spawned in the rivers; today perhaps 15,000,000 salmon—most of them from hatcheries—travel down to the ocean. One hundred seven stocks of salmon have become extinct in the Pacific Area, 89 others are at risk.

The Bonneville Dam on the Columbia River to the east of Portland covers the Yakima's treaty land and fishing grounds from the dam to above The Dalles. The Falls of the Women's Hair (Tixni)—also on the Columbia River—is the geographic heart of the Salmon Culture. Today it is spanned by The Dalles Dam Complex.

The Bonneville Power Administration has been judged in violation of the Endangered Species Act and has been required to make drastic changes. Native Americans of that area feel that waters from the dam should be "released according to the salmon's schedule, not according to the electricity demands of the aluminum companies."[6]

In an effort to increase the salmon stocks, the Yakimas—to the northeast of the Dalles—even tend fish in the cooling ponds at the Hanford Nuclear reserve in Washington. (The Hanford Nuclear plant is the largest source of radioactive contamination in the area.) More than 500,000 Chinook salmon reared this way (and that have tested free of radio-nuclides) are being released into the river.

"They are our hope," says Jerry Menick, Yakima Tribal Chair, "they are our future. If the salmon survive and return to spawning in the Columbia, we may again someday have a real harvest."

And so even through hardships and disruptions, the Pacific Coastal people have kept their sense of who they are and who their ancestors were. They have become well organized politically and, though small in number, are fighting to save the dwindling natural resources—the old-growth trees, the salmon, and the purity of their water—which are the very roots of their culture!

A TALE OF INTRIGUE AND DESPAIR AMONG THE TLINGIT

In the early 1800s an important Tlingit leader at the village of Klukwan had a master carver create four house posts and a screen to be displayed under the Whale crest in a tribal house. (Although his people had no written language, they could read their history from these carvings.) The screen, known as the Rain Wall, and the house posts have been traditionally recognized as the most exquisite and desirable carvings on the

Northwest Coast. Anthropologists and museum collectors spent years trying to obtain these pieces, but clan members refused to part with the mythic treasures.

In the 1970s a Seattle art dealer tried to buy the carvings; at first he offered $100,000 for them. He met with tribal resistance and disagreement as to who actually "owned" the pieces. Whale clan members agreed to sell and then changed their minds. Then the Klukwan tribal council ruled that artifacts could not be sold without the permission of the council. The dealer persisted and in 1984 the Whale House family agreed to sell the screen and posts (which were to be placed in a major museum) for $1,000,000!

On a Wednesday night in April, when most of the villagers were away playing bingo, the Whale House was unlocked, the carvings loaded into pick-up trucks, and then driven to the town of Haines. Soon they were on a ferry to Seattle where they were put into a warehouse.

When the people of Klukwan realized what had happened, they called the Alaska State Troopers, who eventually traced the pieces to Seattle. The Tlingit tribal council began legal proceedings to stop the sale of the carvings and have them returned to Klukwan.

Almost a decade passed before the case was settled. In November 1993 Judge James Bowen—a Klallam Indian from Washington state—ruled that the art belongs to the entire clan (not just to the one family charged with its care-taking) and should, after 10 years in storage, be returned to the Whale House. He also ordered the dealer to pay $200,000 in village legal costs. The art dealer said that the legal fees involved in fighting the case had financially ruined him. In June 1994 everyone involved in the case signed legal papers that returned the carvings to Klukwan. The dealer agreed, basically, never to contact the clan again and, in return, the village dropped its claims against him for the legal fees.

And so their treasures were returned to them amid ceremonial dancing and prayers.[7] (See Photo 41.)

As David Katciek, a Juneau Tlingit raised at Klukwan, expressed, "They're not just pieces of art, they're things that tell the history and struggle of our community. We're bringing our heritage and our culture back to our community," he said, near tears. Then motioning to his young daughter, "This is who we are doing it for." (See Photo 42.)

TO WALK IN TWO WORLDS

"To walk in two worlds in one spirit. To hunt caribou and then sit down at a computer, to sew mukluks and later balance a checkbook—to remain Inupiat in a world of modern technology. The odds against striking such a balance are steep, but then thousands of arctic winters have bred into The People a talent for survival. They may just pull it off."

—*The Last Light Breaking, Living Among Alaska's Inupiat Eskimos,*
Nick Jans, 1993, Alaska Northwest Books, Anchorage

Ninety percent of Alaska is still a roadless wilderness of tiny villages adrift on a sea of land. The Inuit of today lives in two worlds, perhaps belonging to neither one. He travels by snowmobile, not dog sled, plays basketball in the school gym, watches TV instead

Photo 41. Rainwall screen, 1895. *Courtesy Smithsonian Institution.*

Photo 42. Tlingit Whale House, 1895. *Reproduced from collection of The Library of Congress, Washington, D.C.*

of listening to the old tales in a sod building. He lives in a pre-fab house in a town with a school, a store, a public health center, and a handicraft industry or cannery.

For at least the last 30 years Eskimos have lived in settled communities. For 20-some years, the Alaskan natives knew abundance because of the Alaska pipeline subsidies. Sometimes present-day Inuits have to fall back on welfare (in the form of federal checks or food stamps) to keep their family going.

You can learn another aspect of contemporary Alaskan life by looking in on an Inuit family at dinner time. On their table you may see store-bought Campbell's soup, crackers, soda and canned peas, but these are always supplemented by food from the land: caribou meat, dried salmon, beluga muktuk or frozen trout with *usruk*, the seal oil that "goes with everything." Dessert may be berries or *kutuq*, Eskimo ice cream made of whipped fat mixed with sugar, berries, and boiled fish. The evening menu depends on the season and how lucky the hunters have been, but the meal always includes some foods from the land.

Alaska has gone through many periods of boom and bust—abundance followed by times of poverty. Today the oil money has dwindled. School budgets have been slashed at all levels, but student achievement continues its slow steady improvement with each year.

To walk in two worlds in one spirit—this is the challenge faced by each Native American today.

Notes for "The Coastal Indians Today":

1. The following are the Native American population numbers for the Pacific Coast states, according to the 1990 U.S. census:

   - *California* ranks second among states in American Indian population with 242,164—about 1% of all the people living in the state. More than half of these native people live in Los Angeles (87,487) and San Francisco (40,847). One hundred three American Indian Nations (federally recognized tribes) are located in this state.

   - *Oregon* ranks fourteenth in American Indian population with 38,496—about 1½% of the state's total population. Some 5,000 of these Native Americans live on reserves east of the Cascades. There are seven recognized American Indian Nations in Oregon.

   - *Washington* ranks fifth among states in American Indian population with 81,483—about 2% of the state's total population; 32,017 of Washington's Native Americans live in the Seattle-Tacoma area. There are 27 federally recognized tribes in Washington.

   - *Alaska* has 85,698 Eskimo, Indian, and Aleut people living in the state. This is about 15 ½% of Alaska's total population.

Total statistics vary from source to source. For further research, call the U.S.
Bureau of the Census/Education Program at 301-763-1510 and ask for the catalog and teaching supplement for grades 5-12: *Statistics Aren't Static.*

American Indian and Alaskan Native Areas (a list of reservations and American
Indian population numbers) is available from the U.S. Bureau of the
Census/Racial Statistics, Population Division at 301-763-4040.

The Federal Register of Recognized Tribes is available from the Bureau of Indian
Affairs/Tribal Services at 202-208-7445.

2. As of April 1996 gambling on Indian lands was a $4 billion-a-year business in the
United States; there were 126 such casinos in 24 states. Many states are challeng-
ing The Indian Gaming Regulatory Act, the Federal law that allows Native
Americans to set up gambling businesses on their lands. The U.S. Supreme Court
will have to resolve these conflicts.

3. For information on California Indians, write to: California Department of
Education, P.O. Box 944272, Sacramento CA 94244-2720.

4. California has the largest number of endangered languages in all of North America.

"Beautiful languages in which are encoded the wisdom and poetry of a people
are today reduced to a handful of elderly speakers. With the founding of organizations such as *Advocates for Indigenous California Language Survival*,
through master/apprentice [programs]...many who saw the passing of their
languages as inevitable have now been given hope."

—*News from Native California*,
January 20, 1993, page 5, Malcolm Margolin, Publisher

"As for myself I had the distinct sense that I was bringing the songs back to life.
I also felt that they must be nursed along, for they were somehow weak, and
easily bruised. I don't believe I was alone in this feeling."

—Julian Lang, Karuk writer, lecturer,
archival researcher in the San Francisco Bay Area

5. Quoted from the article "Pesticides and Basketry" by Bev Ortiz, published in *News
from Native California, an Inside View of the California Indian World*, vol. 7,
no. 3, Summer 1993, page 7.

6. Some of the references are from "Salmon People: Susanna Santos," an article by
Winona Laduke (Ojibwe) in *Indigenous Women* (a publication of the Indigenous
Women's Network), vol. ii, no. 2, January 20, 1995.

7. From *The Anchorage Daily News*, October 14, 1994, "Clans Artifacts Returned,
Klukwan Celebrates End of Legal Battle" by Marilee Enge.

But not everyone celebrated. The family that most recently claimed to own and
control the Whale House has not agreed to cooperate in making decisions about the
future of the house and its crest art. At present the citizens of Klukwan are trying
to decide if the pieces should become part of a Village Cultural Center and, if so,
how to raise funds for such a building. (See Photos 43 and 44.)

Photo 43. Contemporary Haida (Masset) Town Center. *Courtesy Robert Easton, photographer.*

Photo 44. Contemporary Haida Council House, Skidegate. *Courtesy Robert Easton, photographer.*

HISTORIC NATIVE AMERICANS OF THE PACIFIC COAST STATES

ISHI (C. 1862-1916)

Ishi was a Yana Indian. The Yanas were a small band of people who lived in the woods to the east of the Sacramento River between Mill and Deer creeks. In their language "yana" means "the people."

Ishi's first memory of non-Indians was of a raid on his village when whites killed his father and other people of his tribe, stealing their possessions and destroying their village. Ishi and the others went far back into the Deer Creek forests, and lived and hid there for many many years.

Ishi learned the ways of his tribe, the old songs and stories and dances. He gave thanks and prayed for protection. Though there weren't many people in his group now, they worked together to stay alive. In the summer they caught deer, fish and rabbit, and dried them for the winter. In fall they gathered acorns and made them into flour which they stored in their handmade baskets. Ishi lived in the sweat house with the men in the summer; in the winter, he lived with his mother in her earth-covered house.

Then one day after almost forty years some white men found the Yanas' little camp. Ishi and the others fled into the forest to hide. The men were surveyors; they looked around the camp and found a very old woman who was too sick to have run away. They didn't bother her but they stripped the camp of all its handmade objects: they stole all the bows and arrows, the baskets, the rabbitskin blankets, and all the tools. When Ishi and the others finally returned they realized how hard it would be to remake all their blankets, baskets and tools *before* they died of hunger or cold.

One by one the few Yanas died until only Ishi and his mother were left. Then she also died. Ishi honored her with songs and sacred tobacco smoke; he painted his face with stripes of sorrow; he burnt off his hair which was the Yana way of mourning the loss of a loved one. Then Ishi wandered away and kept on wandering for three years until one day in August of 1911 he was found huddled next to a barn near Oroville. He was placed that night in the jail for his protection and in the morning anthropologist Thomas Waterman of the University of California came to see Ishi.

Waterman asked Ishi what his name was—but this was such a direct and personal question to a Yana that the Native American did not answer. So the anthropologist named the thin Yana man Ishi, the Yana word for "person" or "one of the people."

Ishi went to San Francisco where he was given a pleasant bedroom and sitting room at the museum. For months Ishi met with Waterman and another anthropologist, Alfred Kroeber, who both wanted to learn all they could about Ishi's language and his ideas.

Each Sunday Ishi showed the visitors how his people made a bow, an arrowhead or even a house. At first the crowds were too much for him, as in the forest he had never seen more than 25 or 30 people together at one time. Slowly Ishi grew more comfortable with his new life. He wore suits like Dr. Kroeber and Dr. Waterman as this was the polite thing for a guest to do in his culture (mirror the actions of one's hosts), although he never learned to enjoy wearing shoes.

In time Ishi learned 600 English words but he was careful not to say a new word until he could pronounce it correctly. Sometimes out of kindness he purposely mispronounced a Yana word in order to make it sound more like the anthropologists' way of saying it.

In the spring of 1914, Ishi went back to the lands of the Yana with the two doctors and two friends. What a joyous time! Ishi shared his earlier experiences with them: he snared and dressed a deer; made a salmon harpoon and a bow, pointed out a good fishing hole and the place where he had killed a deer. Together they lived as the Yanas had lived. Dr. Kroeber wrote down everything. After some weeks Ishi was ready to go back to the museum, the place he now called home.

At the end of the year Ishi came down with tuberculosis and—when he died two years later—his friend Dr. Kroeber said of Ishi,

> "He was the most patient man I ever knew. ...He had mastered the philosophy of patience without a trace of either self pity or bitterness to dull the purity of his cheerful enduringness."

With the death of Ishi the world lost a kind, sensitive, thoughtful spirit...as well as the very last Yana.

SACAJAWEA (C. 1786-1812?)

One day in about 1800 (in present-day Idaho) the Minnetarees attacked a Lemhi-Shoshoni village in the Rocky Mountains. During the raid the Shoshoni chief was killed and his daughter, Sacajawea (sac-uh'juh-WE-uh), was kidnapped. The raiding party took the girl back to their camp in upper Missouri. Sacajawea missed her family, but she always hoped she'd eventually return to them.

After some time the Minatarees traded or sold her to the Mandan tribe of North Dakota. Sacajawea spent the next three years working in their fields.

Then one day a French trader named Charboneau (SHAR-bon-no) bought her and made her his wife. She was now about seventeen.

In the fall of 1804 there were sixteen U.S. states, all of them east of the Mississippi River. That year the Great White Chief, Thomas Jefferson, the third United States President, wanted to have the rest of this continent explored and maps made. He wanted to know all about the plants and animals and people who lived throughout this land. He was hoping a waterway would be found from the Missouri River to the Colorado River.

Jefferson chose two men to lead the exploring party in the West: William Clark and Meriwether Lewis. They, in turn, hired Charboneau to be their guide on the journey. Sacajawea, who had a one-and-a-half-month-old baby, went on the trip, too.

They headed up the river to try and find the Shining Mountains (the Rockies), cross these, and reach the Pacific Ocean.

It was a long hard trip. They saw wolves, buffalo, wildcats, eagles, wild geese, and bear. The men brought game back to camp and Sacajawea got wild berries and roots—only she knew the ones that were good! There were many dangers: poisonous snakes, unfriendly people, floods, and roaring winds. At night Sacajawea mended the men's clothing and moccasins by the light of the fire.

Sacajawea taught Lewis some sign language and some Shoshoni to help him "speak" with the Indians.

One day they saw the white peaks of the mountains shining across the distance! Sacajawea thought, "Soon I will see my people again!" But now the river got wild! There were huge waterfalls; at one point the canoes overturned and all the notebooks and journals floated away down the river! Sacajawea swam out into the icy waters and saved the records from being lost!

Once they had reached the Shining Mountains they needed horses to continue the trip. Lewis and his men went ahead and asked the Shoshoni to sell them some horses, but the Indians refused. Then Captain Clark and Sacajawea came into the camp and the Lemhi-Shoshoni at once recognized her! In fact her brother, Cameahwait, was now their chief! Sacajawea was *so* happy to see her people again! She convinced her brother to sell the exploring party the needed horses.

Eventually the party hid their boats and rode their horses over the mountains. Sacajawea rode also, with her little son, Pompe, on her back. They faced snow, hunger and cold, but finally they crossed the mountains! They left their horses with friendly Indians, made boats, and took off down the river.

Whenever they met Indians, and sometimes these people were not friendly, Sacajawea would speak with them and reassure them that the explorers were not dangerous.

Twice on the trip Sacajawea pointed the way through difficult passes.

Finally the group entered the Columbia River which took them to the sea. In November of 1805, Lewis and Clark raised the U.S. flag claiming the Northwest for the United States.

Because it was now winter, they could not make their return trip at once, so Sacajawea spent a pleasant three months on the coast. She even got to see a beached whale!

After many months the group did return safely to the Mandan village in North Dakota; Charboneau, Sacajawea, and Pompe stayed there while Lewis and Clark went on to Washington to report to President Jefferson.

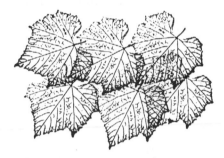

We are not sure what became of Sacajawea. Some say she died on December 20, 1812, but other accounts tell that she returned to the Shoshoni to live for many years—maybe to the age of 100 years old! The real story of her death will probably always be one of history's secrets.

SEATHL: DUWAMISH CHIEF AND PEACEMAKER (C. 1788-1866)

Seattle, Washington is the largest United States city to be named for a Native American. It was given this name to honor a chief who showed real friendship toward white people and who made wonderful speeches.

His name was Seathl. He lived in a village off Puget Sound; his people were fishermen who carved sleek dugout canoes that they used for travel, fishing, and warfare.

Seathl

When Seathl was only four, in 1792, a "white-winged bird ship," the Discovery, captained by English explorer George Vancouver, sailed by his homeland. This was the first time the white men had been seen by native people in the Pacific Northwest. After that, more and more of these white strangers came and even settled in that part of the country. Among these were French Catholic missionaries, who arrived in the 1830s.

Seathl listened to the priests and at last he became a Christian. He had by now become a chief and Seathl always tried to be a peacemaker. When the white settlers came and made a town on the east side of his lands, in what is now the middle of Seattle, he welcomed the newcomers. Their settlement grew fast and in 1852 it was given the name of Seattle to honor the kind chief.

After a while, as more and more people moved there, trouble between the native peoples and the settlers began to grow. Seathl was the first Northwest native leader to sign a treaty, the Treaty of Port Elliott, to try and stop the bad feelings between the two groups of people. But the fighting continued.

At last Seathl even moved with his people to a reservation on the western side of Puget Sound, where he lived in a huge community house (60 by 900 feet). It was here he spent the rest of his life.

Seathl was a tall strong man who had a deep voice that carried well in a crowd. All through his life he made speeches to help bring people together. In 1854 he made a speech to Governor Stevens when he was visiting the city of Seattle. There was a white translator in the audience who wrote down the speech as he heard it; the translation may not be exactly the words that Seathl spoke, but Chief Seathl's feelings shine through even today! Here is a section of that speech:

"Every part of this soil is sacred in the estimation of my people. Every hillside, every valley, every plain and grove, has been hallowed by some sad or happy event in days long vanished. The very dust upon which you now stand responds more lovingly to their footsteps than to yours, because it is rich with the blood of our ancestors and our bare feet are conscious of the sympathetic touch. ...When the last Red Man shall have perished, and the memory of my tribe shall have become a myth among the White Men, these shores will swarm with the invisible dead of my tribe, and when your children's children think themselves alone in the field, the store, the shop, upon the highway, or in the silence of the pathless woods, they will not be alone. At night when the streets of your cities and villages are silent and you think them deserted, they will throng with returning hosts that once filled and still love this beautiful land. The White Man will never be alone. Let him be just and deal kindly with my people, for the dead are not powerless. Dead, did I say? There is no death, only a change of worlds."

CHIEF JOSEPH: NEZ PERCE PATRIOT AND RESISTANCE LEADER (C. 1840-1904)

Chief Joseph

The Nez Perce were a group of native peoples living in easternmost Oregon and Washington, and in the adjoining part of Idaho. Before the coming of the white men they fished for salmon and hunted game, but by the 1800s they were famous for their fine herds of horses.

For many years the Nez Perce were friendly with white people. The Lewis and Clark expedition visited their area in 1805; trappers, traders, and Christian missionaries came through their lands. By the 1840s many homesteaders were moving into eastern Oregon and Washington. As the settlers took more and more land away from the Indians, fighting began.

There was a band of Nez Perce people who had always lived in the rich green Wallowa valley in Oregon. Their chief's given name was In-mut-too-yah-lat-lat, "Thunder Coming Up Over The Land From The Water"; this man was Chief Joseph. For years the U.S. Government kept trying to move his people out of their valley; Chief Joseph always tried to keep the peace even as he refused to move away "from where the old ones were buried."

At last in the spring of 1877 the U.S. Government got ready to force the Nez Perce out of the Wallowa valley; a few young native men got into a fight with some white settlers and ended up killing them. The army sent troops to capture the young men and any other troublemakers. Chief Joseph urged his people to stay calm, but some of the band fought off the army troops. Now Chief Joseph saw that all hope of living peacefully was gone. They were at war and they were completely outnumbered. They must leave their beloved valley. They must flee to the buffalo lands of Montana. They did...with the U.S. Army right behind them. This went on for four months.

There were weeks and weeks of forced marches and fighting in rugged country; as more and more of their people were wounded or fell sick, travel grew more and more difficult. Chief Joseph guided them to the north, hoping to escape into Canada, but winter was coming on; food was growing scarce, and his people were exhausted. Then just 30 miles from Canada they were attacked by fresh army troops. The battle lasted five days. At last on October 5, Chief Joseph was forced to surrender. He met with headmen and scouts of General Howard and an army officer (Lieutenant C. E. S. Wood) wrote down what he said; although there are several slightly different versions of this speech, the heartfelt sentiments of Chief Joseph are shown in each.

Chief Joseph's Speech of Surrender

Tell General Howard I know his heart. What he told me before I have in my heart. I am tired of fighting. Our chiefs are killed. Looking Glass is dead. Too-hul-hul-sole is dead. The old men are all dead. He Who Led the Young Men is dead. My people, some of them, have run away to the hills, and have no blankets, no food. No one knows where they are—perhaps they are freezing to death. I want to have time to look for my children and see how many I can find. Maybe I shall find them among the dead.

Hear me, my chiefs! I am tired. My heart is sick and sad. From where the sun now stands, I will fight no more forever.

Behind Chief Joseph came his beaten people—87 warriors, 40 of whom were wounded; 184 women and 147 children, sick, hungry, and freezing; and 1,100 starving horses.

During their 1,700-mile march over rough lands and without much food, their 350 warriors had held off 2,000 army troops, fought 11 battles, and killed 350 soldiers.

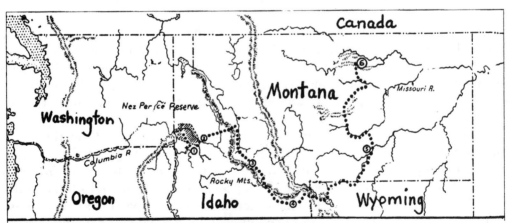

Retreat of Chief Joseph and the Nez Perce ·· ·· ···· July 11 - Oct. 5, 1877
—and the 6 main battle sites—

Of these people, General William Sherman said,

The Indians throughout displayed a courage and skill that elicited universal praise; they abstained from scalping, let captive women go free, and did not commit indiscriminate murder of peaceful families, which is usual, and fought with almost scientific skill.

Chief Joseph and his people were promised that they would be sent to a reservation in Idaho, but instead they were sent to Kansas and later to Oklahoma where they were told to become farmers. They were hunters, not crop growers, by nature. Many died of malaria or starvation.

Joseph tried every way he could think of to get the U.S. Government to let the Nez Perce return to the lands where their ancestors were buried. He traveled twice to Washington, D.C. to explain his ideas and make his pleas. In 1885, Joseph and most of the Nez Perce were sent to Washington state, to a place very different from their beloved Wallowa valley. And that is where they were kept. When Chief Joseph died, the reservation doctor reported that his death was caused by a broken heart.

OTHER IMPORTANT NATIVE AMERICANS FROM CALIFORNIA

Irataba, Mojave chief and visionary

Mabel McKay, world-renowned Pomo basketmaker

Essie Parrish, Pomo ethnographer, spiritual leader, and award-winning filmmaker: *Shaman, Beautiful Tree*

THE
COASTAL INDIANS
Activities for the Classroom

CRAFTS AND CLAY FUN

These craft-making suggestions have been included because each provides a sense of what it was like to deal with situations met by early people; each craft is educational *and* fun to do, and is possible to complete in a relatively short amount of time.

Sand Clay Recipe

This is a terrific recipe for clay as it produces a material that is easy to form and clean; it is fast drying and, once dry, rock hard! This recipe will provide a lump each for 10+ students. You will need:

2 cups sifted sand
1 cup corn starch
1 1/2 cups cold water

Use a heavy pan that you buy at the Goodwill (as sand would be hard on your cooking pan) and get a sturdy wooden spoon to use for stirring. Cook the 3 ingredients over medium heat, stirring constantly for 5 to 10 minutes until mixture is very thick. (When doubled, the recipe produces a mixture that, near completion, may be difficult to stir.) Turn clay out onto a plate and cover with a damp cloth. Cool. Knead the clay 2 or 3 times when it is cool enough to handle.

Sand clay should remain moist. It may be kept overnight if double-bagged in plastic (tightly wrapped and tied off). Knead 2 to 3 times before use.

A Three-Dimensional Map

Cooked Salt Dough

This dough is well-suited for making three-dimensional maps. The following recipe will provide enough dough for 10 to 12 students (5 to 6 maps).

You will need:
6 cups salt
3 cups corn starch
3 cups water

Cook over medium heat, stirring constantly until just stiff. Don't overcook dough or it will become brittle. Make enough dough for your entire class. Keep dough moist (overnight) by wrapping *tightly* in a plastic bag. (Allow maps to dry over the weekend.)

Divide the class into pairs so that two students work together on constructing each map. Each pair of students is then given:

a large piece of foam core or heavy cardboard (such scrap pieces are often free from frame shops) a copy of the map from "How the First People Came Here" activity sheet

white glue

toothpicks

2 plastic picnic knives

2 pencils

2 balls of Salt Dough

watercolors or poster paints

Tell the students: "Study the map and, using pencils on your piece of foam core, make a *large* outline of the land masses shown on the map. Next, spread some white glue on the middle area of your drawing to help anchor the clay once it is applied.

"Smooth out one ball of dough onto your land-mass drawing. Stay within the boundaries and smear the dough so that it is thinner near the edges of the map outline and thicker in the interior of the map.

"Now, use the second ball of dough to build up the high areas, the mountain ranges; refer to a topographic map (wall map, globe or atlas) for accurate information. Use the plastic knives and toothpicks to create crevices, rivers, plains, lakes. *Cooperate* in constructing these maps; both of you should be involved in the molding of the map contours.

"Put the maps out of the way (near a heat source) and check periodically to note dryness. Once your map is dry, give it a *light* coat of watercolor; the river and lakes can be painted by using poster paints or watercolor. (Use a toothpick to apply white glue under any area that may have pulled away from the cardboard.) Finally, make a neatly printed title on the foamcore backing; include the signatures of the two cartographers."

Fossils and Prehistoric Creatures

If possible, have actual fossils on display. Make a batch or two of Sand Clay, and wrap it tightly in a plastic bag to keep it moist. Have each child collect small objects to use in their fossilmaking: small shells, feathers, leaves, and bones work very well. A student may construct a small prehistoric animal by gluing some bones, feathers, toothpicks, or balsa wood strips together. Each child gets a lump of Sand Clay and then experiments, making impressions in the clay. Some children may want to build small prehistoric creatures from the clay itself. Remind them to adhere appendages by smearing clay on all the seams, not just "butting a leg against the clay body." A toothpick can be inserted inside the clay to strengthen an appendage or to connect a leg to a body. Let the clay dry well overnight on a cookie sheet near a heat source before moving the student-made fossils.

Pottery

Sand Clay is excellent for making small pinch pots (a ball of clay is pinched in the middle to form the inside of the pot, and the walls of the pot are pinched upward).

Although the people of the western coastal states made little pottery, students can use Sand Clay to replicate steatite (soapstone) bowls, lamps, and Alaskan stoves.

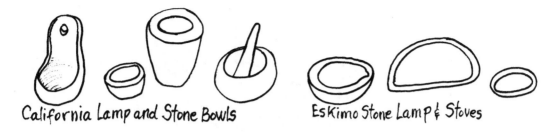

California Lamp and Stone Bowls   Eskimo Stone Lamp & Stoves

Jewelry

You will need for each child: a ball of Sand Clay and a bamboo skewer (packs of these are sold at grocery stores for shish kebabs or barbecues). Give the students time to study the various prehistoric bead shapes you copy onto the chalkboard.

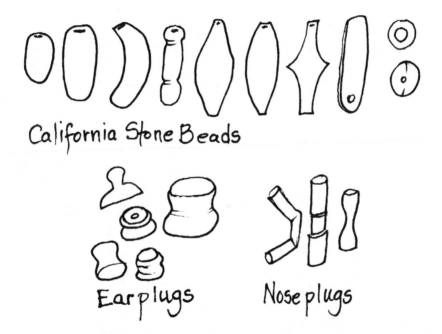

California Stone Beads

Earplugs   Noseplugs

Dentalia shell beads can be formed of the following homemade clay and, once dry, these shell beads can be interspersed between Sand Clay beads on "prehistoric necklaces."

Corn Starch-Baking Soda Dough Recipe

Blend 1 cup corn starch and 2 cups baking soda in a pan. Add 1 ⅓ cups water and stir until smooth. Place pan over medium heat and bring to a boil. Continue to boil for 4 minutes, stirring as you go. Remove from the heat. Stir 2 minutes or longer (the more you stir, the stiffer the dough will be). Cover the dough with plastic wrap and cool for 30 minutes.

Students will roll the dough into 1 ½" to 2 ½" dentalia shells, pierced through with bamboo skewers. These beads may take up to 2 days to dry depending on their thickness. This dough dries pure white and the finished objects can be given a light coat of Verathane if you feel they need added strength.

Mojave Dolls

Study the Mojave dolls of southern California. Have each child mold one of Sand Clay. Make sure that whenever arms and legs are added to the body, they are pressed *into* the body and the seam all around the joint is smoothed down firmly.

Various Mojave Doll Bodies   (‒ ‒ ‒ ‒Joints)

Painted & Clothed Mojave Dolls

Indent all around the eyes and pinch out the ears, lips, and nose from the clay face itself. Use an ice cream stick to indent mouth, fingers, and toes. Use a bamboo skewer to pierce ears.

Allow the dolls to dry thoroughly and then paint them with white, rust, and dark brown tempera paints. Cloth scraps tied on with yarn, and tiny glass bead earrings and necklaces will complete your little Mojave dolls.

SHELTERS

Creative Interpretations of Early Shelters

Provide the students with a variety of materials such as: large sheets of corrugated cardboard (sides of appliance packing boxes), small scraps of plywood, hot glue guns, white glue, ice cream sticks, fine sand, a variety of small boxes (pint juice cartons, little yogurt containers), dried twigs and grass, paintbrushes, milk cartons of different sizes, tempera paints, scissors, construction paper, and <u>Homemade Play Dough</u> (recipe follows).

2 cups flour	2 cups water
1 cup salt	2 Tbsp. salad oil
4 tsp. cream of tartar	food coloring

Mix ingredients together and cook over medium heat until a lumpy soft ball forms: it happens quickly!

Knead a few minutes until dough is smooth. Wrap tightly in a plastic bag to store.

Children can make slabs of play dough and use them to cover the outside of milk or yogurt containers and then press small twigs, dried grass, and fine sand into the covering to simulate brush shelters.

Sand Clay or play dough molded over margarine tubs can replicate the California earth lodge. A twig railing around the outside of the lodge and a stick entrance hall can be added with white glue once the clay has dried.

Ice cream or craft sticks can be glued to low rectangular boxes to create cedar plank long houses. Encourage the students to come up with their own early shelter creations.

When a variety of such miniature shelters has been created, ask for volunteers to form a committee that will be responsible for organizing the student-made shelters into a classroom exhibit. Explain that you will provide any materials they request, free time in which to set up the exhibit, and that they will earn extra credit points (if these are offered in your class).

TOOL-MAKING IDEAS

Get the children to help you collect a good supply of the following: little sticks, dead wooden matches, small scraps of wood, lots of sandpaper, scissors, white glue, markers, thin leather strips, waxed carpet thread, cotton string, small pieces of netting, needles, thread, small round rocks, shells, and long reeds (for atl-atls). A supply of Sand Clay may also be helpful.

Have the students look at pictures of early tools (see **Tools**). Encourage them to bring in specific sticks or pieces of wood, shells, leather, etc., that they think would work well as (part of) a specific tool.

Finally, ask each child to select a tool to faithfully and carefully reproduce (in miniature, if they prefer). Give the class adequate time for this project so they will not feel rushed. Sand Clay may be used for the modeling of stone or bone elements such as bird points, scrapers, arrowheads, hoes, axe heads, and small manos and metates.

When (a selection of) tools have been completed, ask the class to come up with suggestions for exhibiting their work and sharing these handmade tools with other classes. Ask for a volunteer who (for extra credit) will lead the group discussion and oversee the organizing, labeling, and exhibiting of these early tool replications.

Stone Net or Bola Weights   NW Double-Bitted Axe   California Adze Handles   Inuit Slate & Wood Knives

MASKS

Masks are worn for many different reasons: to disguise the wearer, to lend a sense of mystery, to give the wearer the power of the creature the mask portrays. Masks are used to celebrate, to tease, to honor, and to ridicule.

Use library books to study pictures of Northwest Coast or Alaskan masks. Have each student find a mask that he or she would like to replicate. Encourage the child to examine the proportions of the mask and how the features were constructed and then to make a simple drawing of it.

Paper Clay Recipe

(Have the students) tear newspapers into thin long strips. Soak these in water overnight. *Squeeze out all the excess water* from the paper pulp. Rub the wet pulp back and forth between your hands to form a smooth uniform mass.

Put 9 pints of lukewarm water in a plastic pail. Sift 1 pound (one package) of Golden Harvest® wallpaper paste (sold at paint stores) into the water, *stirring* constantly until paste is smooth. Let paste stand for 5 minutes and then add it, little by little, to the paper pulp until a malleable modeling material is created. (Elmer's White Glue-All® can also be added to the pulp to give it strength.) Paper Clay should not be too wet or sticky; if it is, add more paper pulp squeezed quite dry.

Make sure to add enough wallpaper paste so that the resulting Paper Clay will dry hard and not crack or be brittle. It should hold shapes and you should be able to attach small pieces (eyelids, ears, noses) to the basic head shapes without having them come off. (If some appendages should come off, use Elmer's White Glue-All® to adhere them in place again.)

Making the Masks

Each student lays a flattened slab of the modeling material over half a large plastic cottage cheese or yogurt container, as shown in the illustration.

Modeling
Material

large yogurt container
cut in half

Using the mask drawing he or she has made as a guide, the student molds pieces of the clay to form the nose, chin, lips, etc., and attaches them securely to the flattened slab. Then the eyes (and mouth opening) are cut out (using a plastic picnic knife). The

Early Thirties' Imagery
of Northwest Spirit Mask
(Thank you, R.R!)

features of the face should be carefully formed and then the mask should be left to dry, which will take 2 to 4 days depending on its thickness.

Carefully remove the mask from the plastic container and let the underside dry. Use tempera or acrylic paint in historically authentic colors (no lavender, pink, aqua, etc.) to decorate the mask (as shown in library book illustrations).

Eskimo Finger Masks

These little masks were worn by Eskimo women on one or two fingers during ceremonial dances. The little heads were only one to three inches tall. The women made the little masks "carry on conversations with each other" to the delight of the onlookers!

To make these finger masks, you will need: pipe cleaners, posterboard or cardboard, sharp scissors, pencils, (hot) glue (gun), masking tape, small fluffy feathers, and marking pens.

Show the children pictures of some Eskimo finger masks. Have each child draw a little one-inch to three-inch tall face or design on cardboard or posterboard. (You may have to) cut out these little shapes (for very young children). Have them add color to the cut-outs with markers. Each child then takes a pipe cleaner and bends it into a ring that fits a finger rather snugly. Leave both ends of the pipe cleaner straight and tape them to the back of the cardboard shape.

Have each child position little feathers behind the top of their cut-outs and tape [or *you* may (hot) glue] them in place. When the glue is dry, let the children put on their finger masks and make up a little play.

PAPER CLAY TOTEM POLES

To make these very effective group-assembled poles, you will need a tall *heavy duty* mailing tube, a large block of wood about a foot square, a hot glue gun, plastic containers cut in half that fit over the side of the mailing tube (see illustration below), and enough Paper Clay so that each child will get about one cup to use.

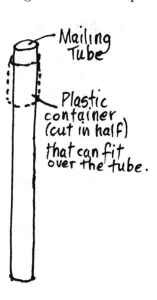

Mailing Tube

Plastic container (cut in half) that can fit over the tube.

Children study photos of totem poles and each models a Paper Clay mask, torso or body over a plastic container half (as described in the previous mask-making project). Once dry, these totem pole parts are assembled and adhered to the mailing tube, using a hot glue gun. After studying color photographs of Northwest crest-poles, the students can paint the pole they have made. When the paint is dry, the totem pole is "raised" and stabilized by using hot glue to adhere it to the wood block.

Collaborative
Crest Pole made by 7 students

PAPER CLAY PUPPET HEADS AND DOLLS

You can use this modeling material to make durable puppets and dolls. Have the students study pictures of early dolls to get ideas for their creations. Painted and dressed, these creations should be lots of fun to use in play *or* in plays. (See illustrations on next page.)

FUN WITH BUTTONS

Contact the thrift stores in your area and ask them to save all their white buttons for your class. Once you have a good selection, use the buttons to provide free-time activities for your young students.

Place the buttons on a serving tray or file box lid. During free time the child can arrange the buttons by size: smallest to largest; by material: shell, plastic, metal; by num-

Ivory Inuit Doll Head   Pacific N.W. Mask Head

ber of eye holes: 2, 4, etc. Ask the child to make up his or her own way of arranging the buttons. Then have other children try to guess the method of arrangement that the child has used. The buttons may be arranged by: color, dark and light values, weight, the uses on clothing with which the buttons are associated, or some specific organization the *child* has worked out. Young children also enjoy outlining their hands or small objects with buttons. When the hand or object is removed, the button outline is revealed! A simple, but satisfying, activity!

Button Blankets

These Northwest blankets were traditionally red and black (or navy) with outlines of crest figures in white buttons (and abalone disks or, occasionally, dentalium shells).

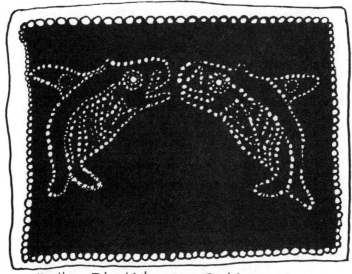

Button Blanket of N.W. Pacific Coast

You will need red and black construction paper, white glue, lots of white buttons (or white notebook hole reinforcers, if buttons are not available), pencils, scissors, and photos of these blankets (collected from Northwest books from the library).

Show several of the photographs to your students and have them make up a short list of ways in which many are similar. Each child then chooses a crest bird, animal, or fish and makes a large simple drawing of it in the middle of a red or black sheet of paper. This sheet is cut down by one or two inches on all four sides and glued flat to the middle of a sheet of a contrasting paper, either red or black.

Finally the child carefully lines up the buttons (or hole reinforcers) next to one another to cover the pencil line, and then glues them into place. Scraps of contrasting paper (red or black) can be cut into little squares and placed at equal intervals along the edge of the paper to make a pattern there.

PETROGLYPH RUBBINGS

For each student you will need: rice paper (sold in rolls at Asian specialty stores and at some art stores) or a piece of old white sheet, masking tape, and (to be shared) black ink pads, roll-on stamp pad ink, several tennis balls (each inside the toe of a rather thin sock), and scissors.

Before making a rubbing, the student should feel the surface of the carved area to be certain that it is deep enough to give a good impression on the paper or cloth.

Next, each child will cut a piece of paper to completely cover his or her petroglyph and will tape the paper tightly in place. The child takes the ball in the sock and firmly taps it against the ink pad until the sock is well inked. This inked sock is then rubbed gently across the paper covering the petroglyph so that it may clearly show where the incised lines occur. The sock will be re-inked when necessary. The child taps the inked sock against the outside edge of each incised line to make the carved picture show up clearly.

Tell the students to step back and look at their rubbings occasionally to make sure they have distinct dark edges along the carved lines and their rubbings are more lightly shaded in other areas.

When a rubbing is finished, the tape is removed and the paper taken off. You now have a unique rubbing AND the petroglyph is left just as you found it!

If you do not have historic petroglyphs in your area, students can still have fun using this technique to create (composite) rubbings of interesting raised surfaces they find in their neighborhood, the classroom, or on the school grounds. (Do be careful with the black ink as it can stain clothing; *Easy-Wash*™ seems to work well with some such stains.)

FOLDED PAPER LONGHOUSE

Each child will need a piece of tan or white 9" by 12" paper and marking pens or crayons.

Show the children how to fold their papers in half crosswise and then take the top flap and fold it in half toward the middle.

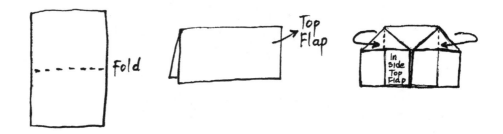

The outside of the longhouse is formed when the paper is folded down flat as shown above. Have the children each draw the cedar planks and doorhole on their paper.

Then when the top flaps are opened out, "we can see inside the longhouse," so have the children draw the inside of the building and the things (and people) we might see there.

"CEDAR" PAINTINGS AND BOXES

Buy some small wooden shingles at the lumber yard and let young children have fun painting on this unusual surface. Older students might transfer a crest figure drawing to a shingle and then paint it using only red, white, and black paints and good (camel hair) brushes; good brushes are essential if we want students to be able to control their paints and not become frustrated by struggling to make plastic bristles produce good lines.

Once older students have painted one to four shingles, they may want to construct "a communally made cedar wood box." Simply use a hot glue gun to adhere six shingles together to form such a cedar box.

FOOD PREPARATION

California

Acorn Meal (for Soup or Cereal)   Acorn soup that is boiled with hot stones has a faint smokiness from the rocks and a warmth of flavor from the woven grasses of the basket; this modern-day recipe will not, unhappily, offer such subtleties of taste, but it's still an interesting endeavor.

Collect the second fall of tan oak acorns. **CAUTION**: Be certain you are actually collecting *acorns*. If you are not positive they are acorns, ask a Science teacher or someone at a plant nursery to identify the nuts before continuing with this recipe!

Fill the bottoms of cardboard soda-carrying containers with acorns. Stir the nuts every day; the cardboard soaks up the moisture from the acorns. (Nuts do dry more quickly if they are shelled first, but they are harder to shell when they are green. Have some of your class try doing it *both* ways!)

Once the acorns are dry, have students shell them and remove the red husk (by rubbing the kernels with the back edge of a table knife). This is done because the husks give soup an unpleasant taste and texture, and, quoting a present-day Native American, "People will say, 'Gee, she's lazy! She doesn't even clean her acorns!'"

Next, grind the dried nuts to a fine powder. Use a mortar and pestle or a hand meat grinder. **CAUTION**: If you use a blender or a food processor, be careful not to burn out the motor! Ground acorns become very dense and, therefore, could be hard on the appliance if the food container is overfilled. Forewarned is forearmed.

Sift the ground nuts. Place the sifted meal in a pillowcase or a new sock. Fill with cool water and let it drain. Tie the sock or case to a faucet so that water drips through the meal all night; this sweetens the flour.

Use a stainless steel pan for cooking; add acorn meal and stir in cool water until it is of a loose consistency. Use a wooden spoon to stir the mixture constantly until it simmers. Turn down the heat and continue stirring for one hour. (During all the cooking time in the old days, prayers were said: "Be sweet for my family. Be a good batch of food to be served well.") Add hot water whenever needed until the soup is like smooth creamy oatmeal. Taste to see that the soup has a pleasant cooked flavor. (Add some cold water to cool soup and stop the cooking process.)

This recipe is based on an article in *News from Native California*, vol. 1, no. 4, September/November, 1987.

I know that lots of times I think "Why do I do this? We don't eat it everyday. Why should I do it?" But. . . it's a special food. It was life to them in earlier years and it is still life to a lot of us who want to learn the ways.

—Julia Parker, Pomo

Chia   Purchase some Chia seeds at a health food store and sprout them in class. The sprouts can be eaten in sandwiches or salads. Stir some Chia seeds, that you have crushed, into lemonade to make a refreshing drink.

Yerba Buena   Pick and dry the leaves of this small shrub. Make sure it *is* yerba buena; if you aren't completely sure, buy some leaves at a health food store. Steep the leaves in boiling water for cups of authentic native tea.

Imi (Pomo Berry Soda)   This is made from berries—blackberries are good—and (sparkling) water. Dried berries are often available at organic specialty stores.

Nearly fill a quart Mason jar with sparkling water and 3/4 cup of dried berries. Leave in the refrigerator overnight. The next day enjoy this refreshing drink.

Pacific Northwest

The basic foods of these early people were fish and seafood, but plant foods were also eaten, including roots and tubers. Here are two Northwest plant foods your students may enjoy.

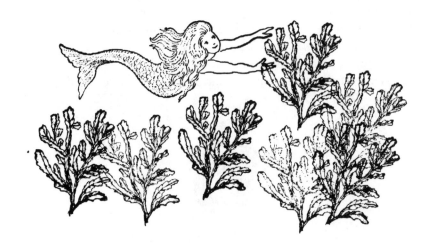

Rosehips   Rosehips are high in Vitamin C. You can buy them or collect these bright red rosehips in the fall. Wash them well. Then they can be eaten raw, made into tea, or used in salads.

Seaweed (Brown Kelp)   Buy dried kelp in the Asian section of a big market or in a health food store. Prepare according to directions. Students may be intrigued by the taste—*or* they may not, but the experiencing is enough!

GAMES

Variations on the following games were played throughout the coastal regions.

Disk Roll (Northwest)

For this game, which can be played indoors or outdoors, you will need 2 short thin sticks (or 3 blocks, if played indoors), a spoon, and 3 to 5 plastic checkers (or golf balls).

   If the game is to be played outdoors, choose a flat smooth area and drive 2 sticks into the ground about one foot apart. Halfway between the sticks dig a 3-inch hole with the spoon. A line is drawn parallel to the sticks 10 feet away.

   Each player rolls 3 to 5 checkers (or golf balls), one after another, toward the goal.

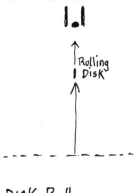

DISK Roll

   The point is to get the checker to roll through the "goal posts" without falling in the hole. The player who gets six points first wins!

   Station one player behind the goal to collect the rolled disks and deliver them back to the players at the 10-foot line.

   If played indoors, two blocks are set up as goal posts and one block between them acts as the "hole." If a rolling disk hits the center block, no point is made.

Stone Drop (Northwest)

For every 5 players you will need a large (5-inch diameter) conch or mussel shell and 15 small (1-inch) stones.

The conch is set on the ground. Each child holds his or her hand out at arm's length and shoulder high and tries to drop a stone into the conch. Each player gets three tries; only the stones that stayed in the shell are counted as points.

What Do I Have?

The class goes outside and disperses, each child picking up and concealing a small natural object (twig, stone, blade of grass, pine cone, feather, bit of tar, etc.).

One after another each child stands in front of the class and extends the hand in which the mystery object is held and asks the class: "What do I have?"

The other children try to guess by asking questions that can be answered "Yes" or "No," such as, "Was it ever alive?" "Is it green?" "Do some birds eat it?" The person who guesses the identity of the object becomes the next standing player. If no one can guess correctly, the player gets a second turn.

Fox, Ducks and Geese (Eskimo)

For this indoor game you will need to have the children model several sets of these animals from Homemade Paper Clay. Each set has 1 fox, 2 ducks, and 2 geese. (The Eskimo children played with animals carved from ivory.)

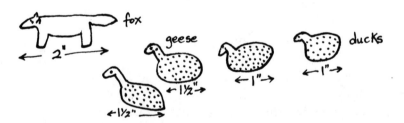

The base of each animal should be thick and flat so that it is stable when put on the floor. (You can imbed a small stone in the base to give the animal weight at its base.)

Each game is played by 2 to 4 players using one set of animals. The first player gently tosses one set of creatures (all at once or one at a time) up into the air from the palm (or back of) her or his hand. Any animal that lands on its base and is left standing is good for points: Fox=5 points, Goose=3 points, Duck=1 point. The score is posted on a running score sheet. The next player takes a turn, and so on, until each player has had five turns, the winner being the player with the most points.

Bump Ball (Alaskan Eskimo)

Inuit children played this game with net-covered inflated bladders from sea mammals. You need 3 light playground balls or small beachballs, all alike except that each one is marked or colored differently. One ball will be the target and should be in high contrast to the others.

The play area will look like the illustration.

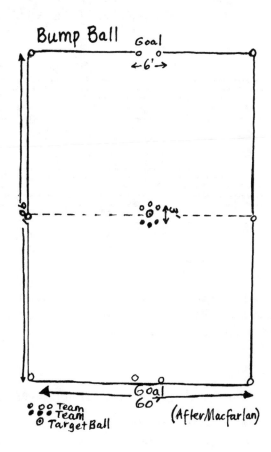

There are just 3 players on each team. At the sound of the whistle, each team throws its own ball at the target ball, trying to drive it toward (and through) the opponents' goal. From here on, players may throw or catch their *own* ball, but they are not allowed to stop or move *any* ball with their feet. The opponents' ball may not be touched—but it can be bumped away by throwing one's own ball at it.

For a faster game, the teams can be given two balls each.

Northwest native children played lone bump ball, practicing driving one bladder ahead of them by driving it with another. Encourage your students to do this in *their* free time!

Lummi Stick Rhythm Game

This is a non-competitive Northwest game, although Eskimos played it using bone "sticks." Playing Lummi Sticks strengthens a child's coordination and sense of rhythm. It has similarities to our games of Pattycake and Jacks.

Two players sit on the floor opposite one another. Each holds a pair of half-inch dowels, 12 inches long, one in each hand. They hold these sticks loosely, upright, with their arms out in the middle of the space between them. To the rhythm of the following song, they perform the patterns described below, matching an action to each beat.

The Lummi Stick Song

Ma Kai ai co ta o ma com tan-ya,

Ma Kai ai co ta o ma com tan-ya.

Young children begin with alternating the first two patterns, one beat after the other. Older students can use the first four patterns at a time, gradually adding more patterns as they grow more skillful.

Lummi Stick Patterns

1. *Down*: Touch floor with sticks in vertical, upright, position.
2. *Together*: Touch sticks together in upright position.
3. *Touch Right*: Tap partner's right stick with your right stick.
4. *Touch Left*: Tap partner's left stick with your left stick.
5. *Throw Right*: Exchange right-hand sticks by tossing across to each other. Sticks must remain vertical during toss.
6. *Throw Left*: Left-hand sticks are tossed vertically.

7. *Throw Both*: Players toss both sticks at the same time. During the toss one pair of sticks should be tossed to the outside and one pair to the inside; sticks are to stay vertical during the toss.

8. *Front*: Hold the sticks horizontally and tap the floor in front of you.

9. *Flip*: Flip your sticks up into the air and catch them by their opposite ends.

10. *Cross*: Hold the sticks horizontally. Cross your hands and tap the floor on opposite sides of yourself.

11. *Side*: Hold sticks horizontally and tap the floor on both sides of yourself.

12. *Up*: Hold up your arms high in the air and, crossing your sticks, tap them together.

INDIVIDUAL HAND-SIZED STUDENT TIMELINES

Here is an excellent way to reinforce historical information you want your class to remember. This technique also aids sequential thinking and is a very good mnemonic device.

You will need: 5" x 8" file cards (three for each student), paper cutter, rulers, pencils, a rubber band for each student, 1-inch wide cellophane tape, markers/crayons, glue, scissors, wildlife magazines, and several table knives.

Preparing the Blank Timelines.

Mark each file card lengthwise at 2⅝" intervals at top and bottom.

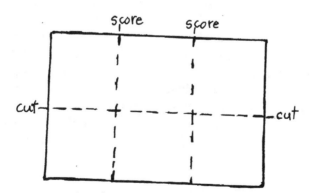

Now use a ruler and the back of the blade of a table knife to connect the first two marks top and bottom; this will score the file card so that it may later be neatly folded.

Connect the second set of two marks with a score line also. (This will create two vertical lines and three columns on the card.)

Then, carefully cut the card in half horizontally. (Each card has now become two 2½" x 8" strips, with three sections in each strip, for a total of six sections.)

Using the Blank Timelines

Demonstrate how to neatly tape two strips (six sections) of a timeline together.

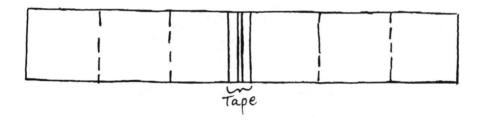

Tape

Each student tapes the two strips together to form the beginning of the individual timeline; then he or she designs an appropriate title section (cover) for the timeline using the words and dates *Native Americans of California,* or *of the Pacific Northwest,* or *of Alaska c. 23,000 B.C. to A.D. 1800).* Each student prints his or her name neatly in tiny letters somewhere on this first section, folds the timeline accordion-like with the cover showing on top, and secures it closed with a rubber band or paper clip.

Collect these blank timelines and return them to the students once you have studied: (1) *c. 23,000-10,000 B.C.: Asian Hunters Cross Bering Strait Into North America.* Each will make a drawing (on the empty section next to his or her title section) to illustrate the Asian hunters coming to North America, and note the date. Collect the timelines and return them to the students after you have studied: (2) *10,000-8,000 B.C.: The Ice Age Ends.* The children each make a picture with magazine cutouts and/or drawings to illustrate the big game hunters in North America. Continue this procedure after the introduction of (each of) the important historical date(s). When five dates have been illustrated, you will need to provide each student with a new index card. Repeat the procedure described above (scoring, cutting, taping) and connect this new part of the timeline to the first part. (Since there are more than eleven sections required to complete

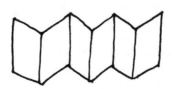

this particular timeline, you will have to go through this procedure once more, later, in order to finish this project.)

Before adding (a) new date(s) to the timelines, have the class quickly read through the dates that have already been noted. Repeating the dates, starting with 50,000 B.C., each time a new date is added will offer good oral review and will help cement the sequential dates in their minds.

Collect the timelines after any new addition is made and store them in a specific place. This protects the timelines and keeps the images fresh for the students.

When the timelines covering the period you are studying are completed, neatly display them (in the hallway) at the children's eye-level, using straight pins or double-stick tape on the *back* (not staples, or tape on the front, which would damage the timelines). This will encourage the students to review the dates as they walk along the hall each day.

Depending on the time you have and the emphasis you want to give the 18th to 20th centuries, you may choose to have the older children make a large classroom timeline: *Coastal Native Americans* A.D. *1800 to 1990.*

Some Dates for Your Timeline

The following dates can be used to make a timeline for the coastal Native Americans.

c. 23,000 B.C.– c. 10,000 B.C.	Time of first people on this continent is unknown. For 1000's of years Asian hunters follow animals into North America over land bridge between Siberia and Alaska.	USA
c. 15,000 B.C. (or earlier)	Del Mar man, ancient Californian (found near Del Mar, CA)	CA
c. 10,000 B.C.– c. 8000 B.C.	Climate changes: Ice Age ends, glaciers retreat, Bering Strait replace land bridge between continents.	USA
c. 9000 B.C. – c. 5000 B.C.	Extinction in North America of mastodons, sabertooth tigers, tapirs, camels, giant armadillos, native horse.	USA
	Cascade Culture people in Oregon—may be ancestors of Pacific Northwest culture.	NW
c. 8000 B.C.	Climate warm enough for coniferous trees.	CA, NW
c. 7500 B.C. – c. 4500 B.C.	Prehistoric bison hunters on the plains; they dry meat, mix it with berries, and store it in hide or gut containers.	USA
c. 6000 B.C.	Deciduous trees grow. Alaskan campsite shows people used stone tools and ate shellfish, seal, sea lion, deer, beaver, and blueberries.	CA, NW, AK
c. 5000 B.C.	Northwest people work wood: shown by the tools found at sites.	NW, AK
c. 4000 B.C.	Footprints (the oldest found in North America) are made by a family as they walked along the Mojave River.	CA
c. 3000 B.C.	Ground and polished stone tools—also bone tools—used in Alaska.	AK
c. 3000 B.C. – c. 1000 B.C.	Eskimo-Aleuts float across Bering Strait from Siberia and settle in Alaska.	AK
c. 500 B.C.	Copper bracelets, weapons, and amulets are made and used.	NW

c. A.D. 1	Large wooden houses in villages in Northwest and southern Alaska.	NW, AK
c. A.D. 500	Bow and arrow used in North America, replacing most atl-atls.	USA
c. 985-1014	Norse (Eric the Red and Leif Ericson) make settlements in North America and meet Eskimos.	AK
1542	The Spaniards Cabrillo and Ferrelo explore Pacific coast.	CA
1578-1579	Sir Francis Drake explores California coast and meets Miwoks.	CA
1725	Peter the Great, Emperor of Russia, sends Vitus Bering to explore the North Pacific.	AK
1741	Vitus Bering and Alexei Chirikof sight Alaska in July. Georg Stellar steps ashore at Kayak Island, becoming the first European to set foot on Alaskan soil.	AK
1761-1766	Aleuts revolt against the Russians.	AK
1769	Portola claims California for Spain and sets up first missions with Father Serra, a Franciscan.	CA
1776-1778	Captain Cook, English, explores Pacific Northwest.	NW
1782-1783	Smallpox epidemic among the Sanpoils of Washington.	NW
1784	Grigori Shelikhov (a Russian) establishes first European settlement in Alaska, at Three Saints Bay, Kodiak.	AK
1787	The Northwest ordinance calls for Indian rights, tribal lands, but leads to more white settlements.	NW
1791-1793	Vancouver, an Englishman, explores the Pacific Northwest.	NW
1799	Alexander Baranov establishes Russian post at Old Sitka.	AK
1802-1867	Tlingits drive out Russians from Sitka in 1802. They continue their resistance for 65 years.	AK
1803-1806	Lewis and Clark expedition to the American West.	NW
1804	Russians return to Sitka; set up new colonial post (at New Sitka).	AK
1812-1841	Russians build Fort Ross on Pomo land in northern California.	CA
1824	Bureau of Indian Affairs (BIA) is organized as part of the U.S. Department of War.	USA
1830	Epidemics of European diseases in California and Oregon.	CA, OR
1843	Russians establish first mission school for Eskimos in Alaska (Greek Orthodox Church).	AK
1844	First commercial whalers in Alaska.	AK
1846	Oregon country becomes part of U.S. as part of settlement with the English.	OR
1847	Measles break out among Cayuse at Presbyterian Mission School, leading to first real violence between Northwest Indians and whites: Cayuse War.	OR
1848-1891	California Gold Rush—beginning of the end for California Indians and their way of life.	CA
1850	California becomes a state.	CA
1850-1851	Mariposa War between miners and Yokuts.	CA

1851	Yuma and Mojave uprising.	CA
1855-1856	Yakima War (Yakimas, Walla Wallas, Umatillas, Cayuses) in response to forced treaties and land takeovers by the U.S. government.	WA, OR
1858	Coeur d'Alene War in Washington, Idaho (Coeur d'Alene, Spokanes, Yakimas, Paiutes): seen as second phase of Yakima Wars.	WA
1866-1868	Snake War (Northern Paiutes, Walpapis).	OR?
1867	U.S. buys Alaska from Russia for 7.2 million dollars.	AK
1869	Transcontinental railroad is completed.	CA, NW
1877	Flight of the Nez Perce under Chief Joseph.	NW
1878	First salmon canneries in Alaska (Old Sitka and Klawok). Bannock War in Idaho and Oregon (Bannocks, Cayuses, Northern Paiutes).	AK, OR
1880	Gold is discovered on Gastineau Channel: Juneau is founded.	AK
1884	First Organic Act for Alaska—begins the withdrawal of large areas of land from native use. Canada outlaws Potlatch Ceremony.	AK, NW
1897-1900	Klondike gold rush in Yukon; heavy traffic through Alaska.	AK
1912	Territorial status for Alaska. Alaskan Native Brotherhood and Sisterhood are founded. (Mt. Katmaiex erupts, forming Valley of 10,000 Smokes.)	AK
1914-1918	*World War I*: Native Americans enlist, fight, and die.	USA
1915	Congress gives approval for BIA to buy land for landless California Indians.	CA
1923	The Alaska Railroad is completed.	AK
1924	U.S. citizenship is granted to all Native Americans born in the U.S. (Indian Citizenship Act)—partly in gratitude for American Indian contributions in WW I.	USA
1936	The Indian Reorganization Act of 1935 is amended to include Alaska.	AK
1941-1945	*World War II*: Native Americans enter U.S. services, and industry. More than 25,000 Native Americans are on active duty.	USA
1947	Tlingit and Haida file first Alaska Native land claims suits.	AK
1948	Alaskans vote to end fish traps by ten to one margin.	AK
1959	Alaska becomes a state on January 3. U.S. Court of Claims judges in favor of Tlingit and Haida in their suit for southeast Alaska lands.	AK
1964	Native Indian Youth Council hold "fish-ins" along Washington rivers in support of Native fishing rights.	WA
1966	Alaskan Federation of Natives is founded: represents Eskimos, Aleuts, and American Indians in Alaska.	AK

1968	Indian Civil Rights Act: gives Native Americans right to self-government on reservations.	USA
1969	Environmental Policy Act protects American Indian resources.	USA
1969-1971	Indians occupy Alcatraz Island in San Francisco Bay to call attention to plight of Native Americans.	CA, USA
1970	Pit River Indians resist development plans of Pacific Gas and Electric Co.	CA
1971	Alaska Natives Claims Settlement Act awards money and forty million acres of land to Native Alaskans.	AK
1972	21,000 acres are returned to Yakimas.	WA
1986	Bill is passed governing subsistence hunting, and fishing.	AK
1988	Indian Gaming Regulatory Act	USA
1990	Native American Grave Protection and Reparation Act: protects American Indian grave sites and requires the return to tribes of identifiable remains, and sacred burial objects.	USA

CREATIVE WRITING (OR JOURNAL ENTRY) SUGGESTIONS

The following may be used as themes for oral readings, creative-writing self-starters, or for collaboratively written pieces.

1. Imagine yourself as one of the first Asians who crosses the Bering Strait into North America. Name several things you see on your walk. What kinds of thoughts do you have? What are you looking forward to? Why will it be a better life for you in this new land? Go into details in your answers; this will make your writing much more interesting.

2. "What's in My House?" (You will begin by printing this question on the board or at the top of a large piece of paper.) The children will then take a few minutes to each make a long list of the many things they see in their own homes. You will assemble a master list containing objects and people mentioned by the children in response to this question.

   Next, ask them to make long lists in answer to the question: "What was in an early California brush house?" (or a Northwest longhouse or an Alaskan half-sunken earth house?) Compile their answers into a group list and have them compare it with the first list they made. Finally, say to the students: "Look back at the (second) list of house furnishings we made. Imagine that you are a coastal Indian. Now write a description of the inside of your home and include some of the things on the list. Add lots of details, such as colors, the number of things, any decorations there may be, who sleeps and works in each part of the shelter, and so on. Make the inside of your home come alive to the reader. (You may want to make a fold-out paper house like the one shown in this chapter to go along with your written piece)."

3. A eulogy is a poem that praises its subject (his or her beauty, nobility, strength and so on). This kind of poem does not need to rhyme. Write a eulogy for the eagle, the whale, or the salmon. Praise many different things about this animal and say why it deserves to have a eulogy written for it.

4. Raven is a creator and a trickster; he is wise and cunning. He makes things happen; sometimes he is too smart for his own good so he ends up being ridiculous. Make up a raven tale to explain how Raven got his pointed nose (beak), or how he brought the salmon to the sea. Or...? Your choice! Have fun!

5. Imagine yourself to be a young coastal Indian child. Think about "your favorite toy," for example, a top, throwing sticks, a doll, bow and arrows, bullroarer, or clay dishes. Make up a short story that includes a detailed description of your toy, who made it, why you first wanted it, why in particular you love it, and how you first learned to use it. Finally, tell what became (or will become) of this special part of your coastal Indian childhood.

6. Study a map that has California, Oregon, Washington, and/or Alaska on it. Think of how you could use different places on the map to tell a story. Maybe you are part of a war party going out to meet the enemy. Perhaps you are a child helping your mother gather food, or you might be a member of a group going to trade with another tribe. Once you have decided on the person you are, make up a story that uses some of the names of places on your map. Include a hand-drawn map that shows everywhere "you" went in your story.

7. In America, getting your driver's license is one way of marking the change from being a kid to being a grown-up. (Think of some other ways we in the United States mark going from being a child to becoming an adult.) What do these ways of marking change have in common? List five or six times in your life that marked a real change in your life during the time you were growing up. Now write a sentence or two about how you were made to feel and what you were thinking on each of these five or six occasions.

8. Brainstorm with your class or with a friend to create a list of experiences that an eagle, bear, salmon, or seal might have. These might include various ways in which the animal might have come in touch with the native peoples, what it thought of humans, and the (mis)adventures that she or he had including what its daily life was like. Use this list to help get a (group) story started. Write your story in the first person and try to make it as original (filled with the unexpected) as you can!

CREATIVE WRITING AND STORYTELLING FOR OLDER STUDENTS

1. Think of the various tools that were made and used by the early people of California, the Pacific Northwest region, or Alaska. Make a quick list of such tools,

including those used for hunting, fishing, food gathering, the making of food, clothing, shelter, or war. Now select three or four tools and write about:

a. how they might have first been invented

b. what their (daily) lives are like (give details)

c. what you imagine their complaints might be

d. what things make them the happiest!

2. *What Is a Culture?* (As a group, reach a collective definition of "culture." Ask the students to each "define one of the cultures from which *you* come." This might be based on ethnic, racial, national, or other roots.) Ask yourself "What are, historically speaking, some general characteristics of this culture? Which of these traits are important to me? What cultural influences have helped to shape the person I am?" Talk together about these questions and their responses—or write about them.

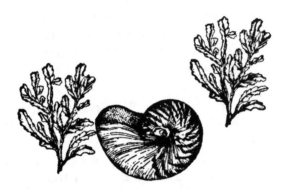

Provide each student with a large sheet of newsprint and a marker. Explain that they have 15 minutes in which to use these to illustrate Coastal Native Americans of California (or the Pacific Northwest or Alaska). They may do this in any way they like: with pictures, drawings, symbols, words, and/or phrases to show what things were important to these people (daily life, art, religion), and what helped to shape these first Americans (climate, geography, etc.).

After 15 minutes each student will tape this piece of newsprint onto the wall of the classroom. Then everyone will take some time to walk around the room, trying to "read" each sheet of paper. Finally, one by one, the students will talk briefly about their drawings and the historical, artistic, religious details shown on these newsprint sheets.

What aspects of *cultural* background show up on these papers?

3. *Creating Northwest Coast Proverbs*:

Ask the students to invent, based on what they know about the culture, some proverbs that these early people *might* have used. Here are some possible examples:

Don't cut down a tree to catch a bird.

Not all trees have the same bark.

A salmon swims upstream only once in its life.

The blubber of a beached whale tastes as sweet as that of one you yourself pooned.

Have the students, as a group, make up some original proverbs and morals like the ones above. Then have them (in pairs) create fables to teach or illustrate these little moral lessons.

4. *Riddle Writing*: Post a list of parts of the body. It might include the following: head, neck, shoulders, arms, elbow, calf, legs, hands, feet, eyes, lip, nose, mouth, temples, palms, wrists, soles, ankles, kneecap, eyelashes, fingernails, muscles, veins, eardrums, heart, stomach, and so on.

All early people made up riddles based on parts of the human body; ask older students to look at the above list and then imagine how a person from the Pacific coast cultures would have made up a riddle about any of the parts of the human body. For example:

What part of the human body is...

A big basket to hold valuables? (**the chest**)

A bunch of rabbits? (**hairs, punning on "hares"**)

A pair of knives straddling a trail? (**shoulder blades**)

You get the idea, and once your students do, they should have a lot of fun riddle-writing!

Following such a writing session, you may ask students to each pick out their best riddle (or three) and share it (them) with the whole class. This should provide a few laughs—or groans!

CULMINATING ACTIVITY 1: CREATING A "MUSEUM OF WEST COAST CULTURE"

When your fourth- to eighth-grade students have completed their studies of Native Americans of California, Oregon, Washington, and Alaska, discuss with them how the class might share with others the things you've made and learned during these last weeks.

If the idea of constructing a classroom museum appeals to the group, start off by making a class-generated list defining a museum and the many things you may find in one. Then have them list all the things they have made during their studies (tools, food, masks, pottery, dolls, timelines, and so on). Help them decide how they might best exhibit these. Finally, organize committees to each take responsibility for a specific aspect of your museum. This might involve categories such as: large signs, labels for exhibits, displays of shelters, the large timeline, and so on; let students come up with the specific categories. Then ask for volunteers for each category (committee) and let these children organize themselves, targeting tasks to be done and how best to effectively complete them. Each committee should make a list of materials they will need to facilitate their work and construct the museum displays. See that the materials are provided.

Next, help them brainstorm how their museum could appeal to all the senses! This could include *taste*: dried fruit, native tea, various sea foods, pemmican; *smell*: cedar, seaweed, leather, smoke; *touch*: objects from the early life of the coastal states, each inside a shoe box with the lid taped shut, and an identifying label in the form of a riddle; *hear*: tape, sound effects, native American instruments; *see*: video, slides, signs, folktale collections; and *make*: replicas, sand clay objects, and so on.

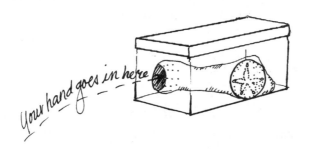

If at all possible, the students should visit a local museum and keep a list of all the physical elements "a good museum" should have: for example, well-written labels and signs, intriguing objects, a clear chronology, thought-provoking exhibits, a few unexpected (hands-on) displays, and so on.

When their museum is completed, invite "the public" and open the doors!

CULMINATING ACTIVITY II: A TIME CAPSULE

Rather than a museum, perhaps your group would like to complete their studies by making a time capsule.

A time capsule is a container made to hold and preserve major elements of a historic time or culture. It is filled and then buried or put into a vault until a much later time (centuries later, perhaps) when it is opened and its contents are studied. Time capsules originated in the 20th century, but let's say that you lived in 1775 in the Coastal states, and on your Vision Quest you were told to create a time capsule in a jar—to show later people what your life was like. What things would you have chosen? Make a list of things that best represent early Californian, Northwest coast, or Alaskan culture. Be sure to include examples of food, clothing, tools, children, arts and crafts, religion, war, and so on.

Make an X-ray picture of the filled jar, as if you were able to see through the sides of the jar and could see all the things in it as well. Show all the details!

At the end of their Native American studies, have the students each list *Five T*
I Didn't Know Before We Studied the Coastal Tribes. You could have them make a sec-
ond list, *Some Things I Still Don't Know About the Northwest Coast Indians...And Wish*
I Did.

As the unit is in progress, you might want to tell your class: "At the end of our
Native American studies, I will want each of you to tell me one thing that you still don't
know concerning the Coastal people, but would like to (have) learn(ed)." This exercise
will help you see where the students' areas of interest lie—and may help you in planning
the "Coastal Indians" unit...for next year!

THE
COASTAL INDIANS

Ready-to-Use
Reproducible Activities

A Note to Teachers about using these Reproducibles

Always make clear to your students WHY you are asking them to complete an activity sheet.

Elicit from the students — or explain to them—reasons for completing a page.

Try to directly connect an individual activity sheet with things you have been discussing or recently doing in class.

These few words of introduction will make EVERY reproducible all the more valuable when your students use it!

HOW THE FIRST PEOPLE CAME HERE

This is a picture of the land we live in: North America.

Long, long ago no people lived here. Ice covered much of the land. The ice made a bridge so people could cross over to the land we live in today.

Many scientists believe that the first people came here from Siberia. Many Native Americans do not believe that their people came here in this way. They believe, instead, the arrival stories of their old songs and myths.

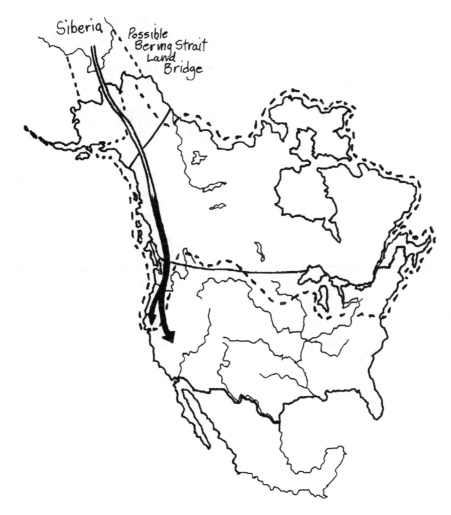

Directions:

1. Use a white crayon to cover all the places the ice covered.
   This is marked by ⌇⌇⌇⌇⌇⌇

2. (Ask your teacher to help you) find where you live in North America.
   Mark it with a ☆

3. Use green to outline the western coastal state(s) that you are studying.

4. Make a long orange arrow to show where scientists think people came from Siberia, through Canada, down to California.

Name _____

A PICTURE COUNT

Count the things you see and put the number in the circle.

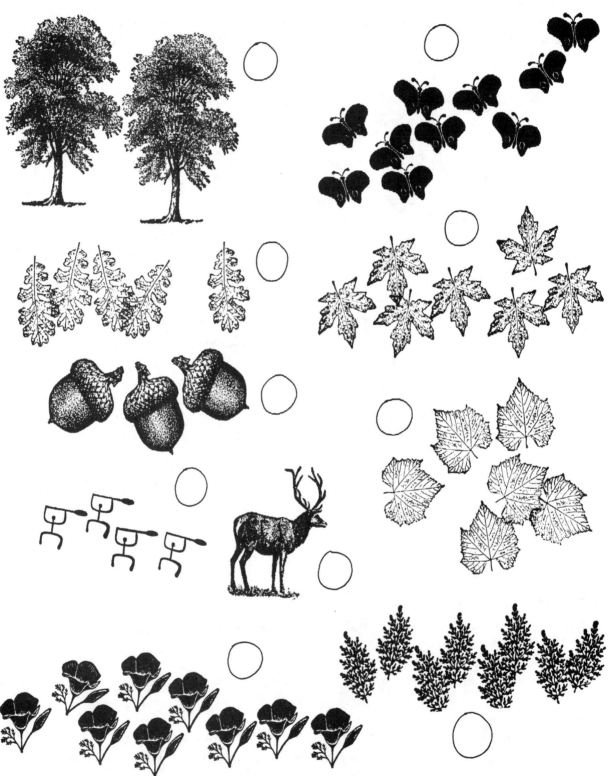

Name _____

A PICTURE COUNT

Count the things you see and put the number in the circle.

Name _____

A PICTURE COUNT

Count the things you see and put the number in the circle.

CAN YOU FIND THE TWINS?

Draw a line between each pair of twins. Then you can color all the twins.

Name _____

CAN YOU FIND THE TWINS?

Draw a line between each pair of twins. Then you can color all the twins.

CAN YOU FIND THE TWINS?

Draw a line between each pair of twins. Then you can color all the twins.

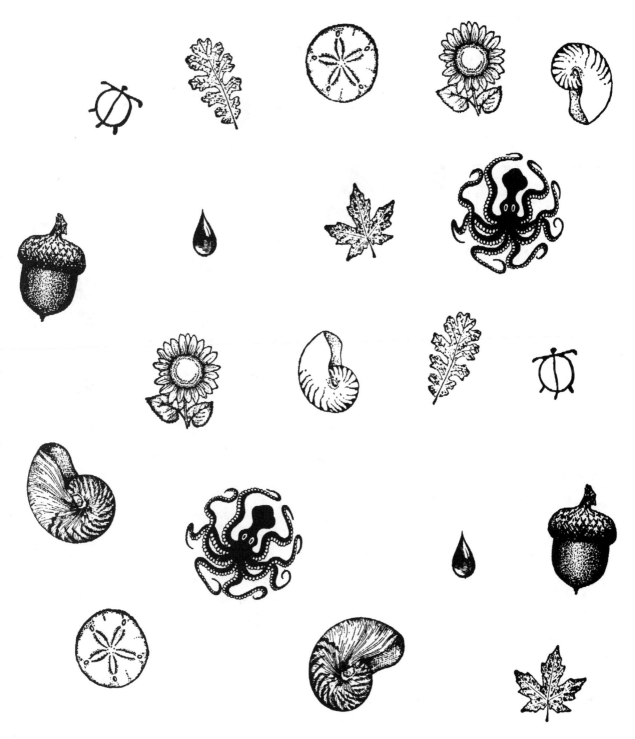

EARLY CALIFORNIA INDIANS CROSSWORD PUZZLE

DOWN

1. ceremonial building (Pomo)
2. used by California Indians to bring down a flying bird
3. plant used to make a skirt in early California
4. "day" in Spanish
7. a safe place
9. important tree to California Indians
10. early baby carrier
12. opposite of "ashamed"
16. "hills" or "mountains" in Spanish
18. California is famous for this
19. plants used to tie poles to outside of plank houses
21. last of the Yana Indians of California

ACROSS

2. a woven grass container
4. boots, each made from 1 log
5. family
6. woven fibers
8. tool used for smoothing wood
11. bird whose red feathers were used by early northern California people
13. seed of the oak tree
14. rocks
15. huge piles of these are by early villages
17. wild onions
20. coastal Indians of central California
22. to take out the bitterness from acorns
23. "bear" in Spanish

CALIFORNIA: THATCHED TULE HOUSE (POMO-YOKUT)

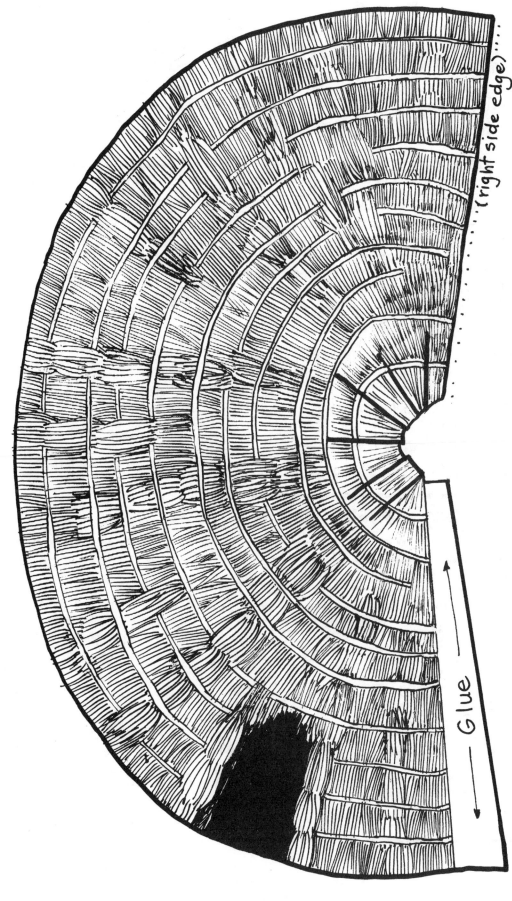

(right side edge)

Glue

Use watercolors or crayons to color the horizontal sticks dark brown and the vertical grasses light green. Cut along the heavy lines. Put glue on the place that says Glue. Swing the glued edge *under* the right-side edge and glue in place. Your thatched tule house is complete!

Northwest Coast Cedar Longhouse, Page 1

Use water colors or crayons to color the longhouse walls and roof: reddish brown.*
Carefully cut along heavy lines and fold back on dotted lines.

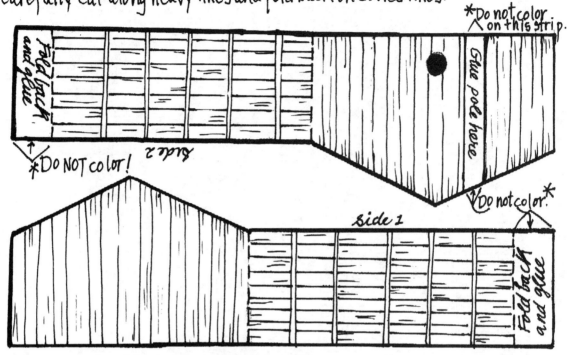

*Do not color on this strip.

Fold back and glue

Glue pole here

Side 2

*DO NOT color!

side 1

Do not color.*

Fold back and glue

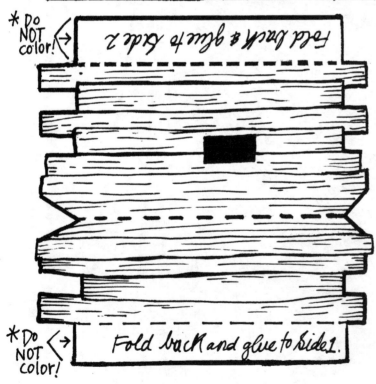

*DO NOT color!

Fold back & glue to Side 2

Fold back and glue to side 1.

*DO NOT color!

Glue the 2 walls together to form a rectangle:

Glue the roof on top of the walls:

(Glue inside)

See Page 2 for Crest Column construction in order to complete your long house!

© 1996 by The Center for Applied Research in Education

Making Crest Columns for your Northwest Coast Long house, Page 2

Color the crest column:

(Glue this edge to make a tube shape)

Glue: to front of long house

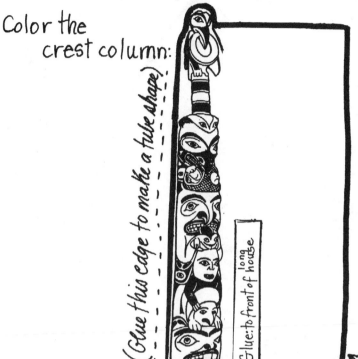

Carefully cut along the heavy lines.

Wrap the cut-out paper tightly around a ball point pen or a long pencil:

Crest Column paper

Unwrap the paper and then glue it so that it stays in a tube shape. Finally glue the column to the longhouse.

completed

You can make your _own_ crest columns with these!

Glue to house

Glue to house

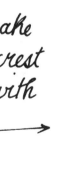

ALASKA: SOD-COVERED WINTER HOUSE, PAGE 1 OF 2

Use crayons to color the grass on your sod-covered winter house: DO NOT color where it says Glue and where it says ENTRY. Carefully cut out the house: cut along the _____ lines. Apply glue to the part that says (1) "Glue." Then swing the part to the right, over onto the glued part. Hold in place until glue dries.

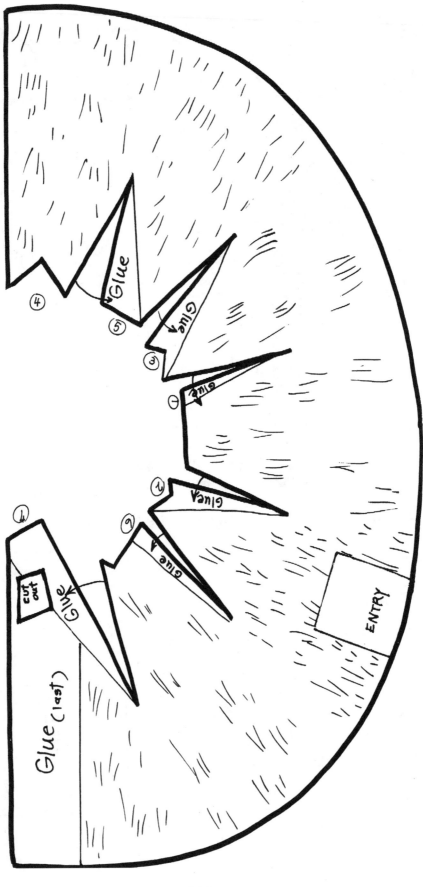

Next, apply glue to (2). Swing (1) over onto the glued part. Repeat these steps for (3) through (6). When they are dry, apply glue to "Glue last" and bring (7) over and place on top of the glued part. Press in place. Trim any loose edges at the top of the lodge. (See page 2 for more instructions.)

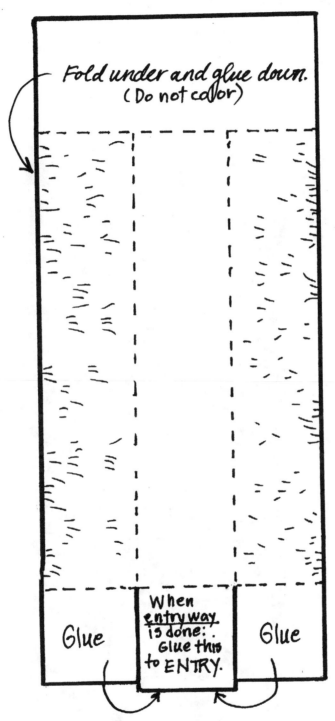

Use crayons to color the grass on this sod-covered entrance hall. Do NOT color where it says Glue or *entry way*.

Cut out the entrance hall along the solid lines. Then fold down along the dotted lines. Put glue on the two corner squares and swing them under the middle square. When your entrance hall is complete, glue it to the entry of your sod-covered winter house. Now your Alaskan Winter House is complete!

Name _____

NORTHWEST INDIAN FOLLOW-THE-DOTS*

Use a pencil. Start at 1. Go on to 2 and keep going until you get to 14!

3·

2·

4·

·5

·6

1·

13·

·

14

12

·7

11·

10·

·8

·9

© 1996 by The Center for Applied Research in Education

*Early Basket from Oregon

Name _____

ALASKAN ABC FOLLOW-THE-DOTS

Using a pencil, start at A and go to B. Keep on going until you get to Z.

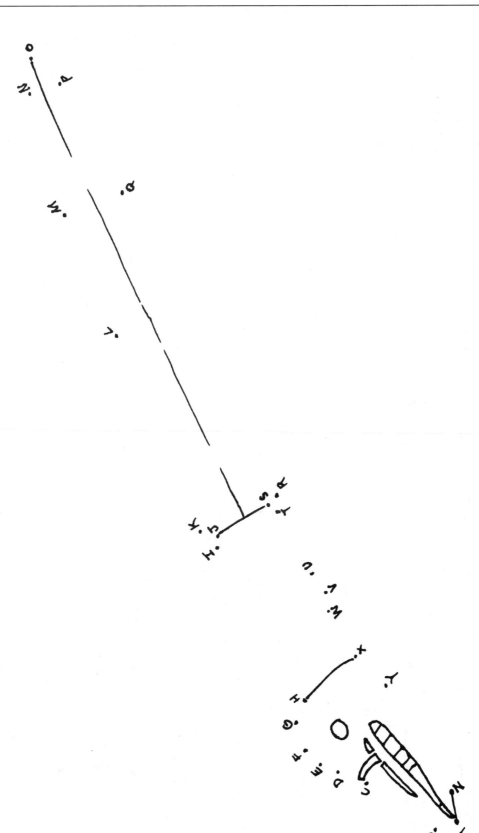

One hundred fifty years ago a Tlingit Indian used this for fighting. Its wooden handle was carved to look like the Raven whose eyes and teeth are inlaid abalone shell.

When you have finished this puzzle, color it carefully.

(SOUTHERN) ALASKA PUZZLE

Use only red, black, and white to color in these (SOUTHERN) *ALASKA PUZZLE* pieces. Then carefully cut out the pieces and try to put them together to make one of my cousins! Good Luck!

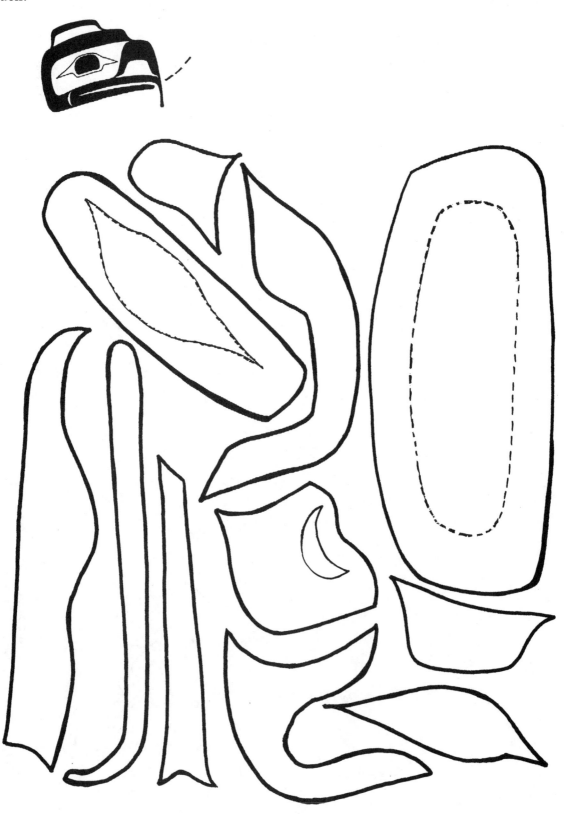

NORTHWEST PUZZLE

Use (R)ed and (B)lack to color in these NORTHWEST PUZZLE pieces. Then carefully cut out the pieces and put them together to make: A KILLER WHALE!

Name _____

CALIFORNIA PICTOGRAPH

This rock painting (pictograph) is in Southern California. Look carefully at it. ...what do you see? ...a person, animals? ...a map? ...a moon? ...a sun?

Write a story to tell WHY this painting was first made. Try to use every part of the pictograph in your story.

Color the pictograph. Use ONLY Earth colors: red, brown, yellow, tan, black, white, and orange.

Name _____

CHILKAT PATTERN BOARD

Men painted half of a design on a cedar board. Then women wove a Chilkat blanket to look like the whole design. A finished Chilkat blanket or robe might be traded and then worn in Washington!

Carefully fill in the empty parts so that it looks like the other half of the design. Make it very exact! Then color it using ONLY: black, white, yellow, and green. Draw a *long* fringe on the bottom of your Chilkat Blanket!

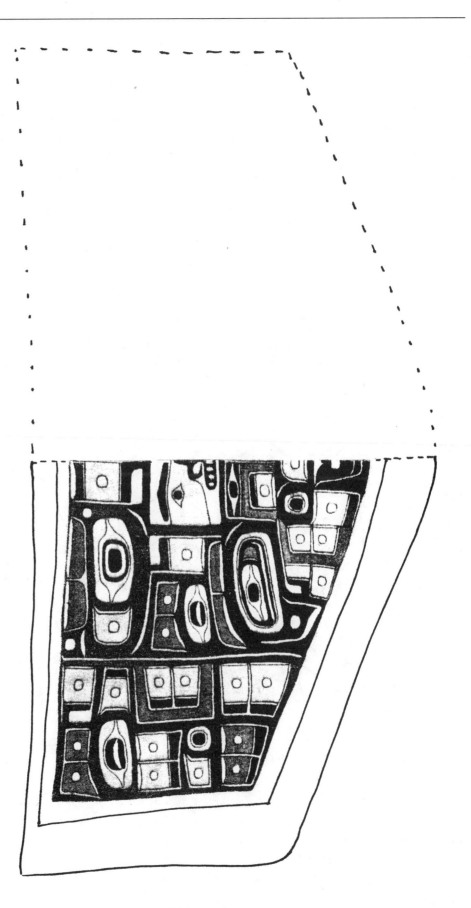

WALRUS HUNT

Carefully color in this Inuit picture:

bl = blue	B = black	G = green
gr = grey	r = red	O = orange
y = yellow	p = purple	w = white

Leave the spots on the walrus and the bird white. Leave the teeth and eyes white, too. Color the faces a very light brown.
(Based on *Four Inuit Catch Walrus*, 1982. Collection of Canadian Museum of Civilization.)

CALIFORNIA INDIAN DOLL AND CLOTHING

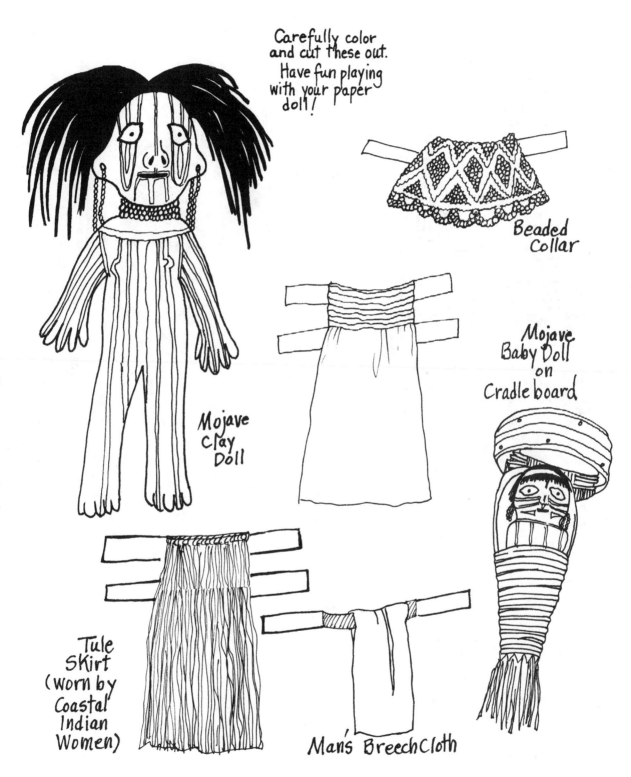

Carefully color and cut these out. Have fun playing with your paper doll!

Beaded Collar

Mojave Clay Doll

Mojave Baby Doll on Cradle board

Tule Skirt (worn by Coastal Indian Women)

Man's Breech Cloth

PACIFIC NORTHWEST DOLL AND CLOTHING

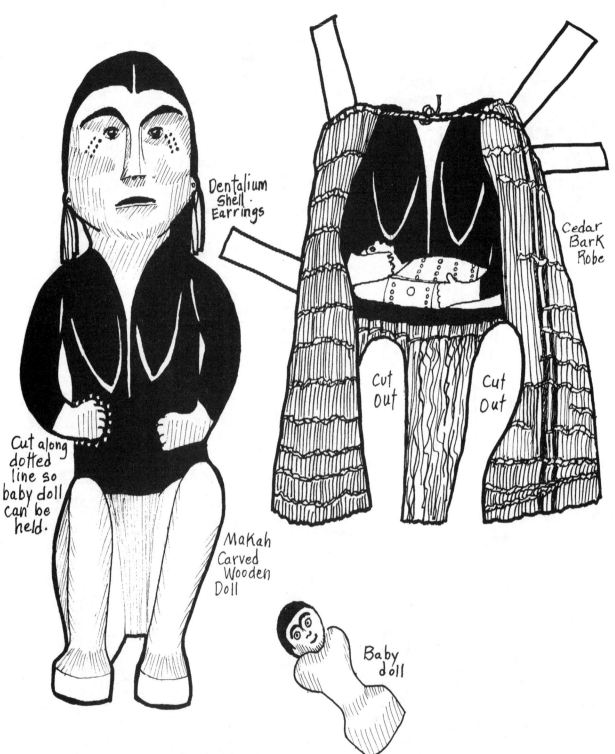

Dentalium
Shell
Earrings

Cedar
Bark
Robe

Cut
Out

Cut
Out

Cut along
dotted
line so
baby doll
can be
held.

Makah
Carved
Wooden
Doll

Baby
doll

Carefully color and cut these things out. (Maybe later you will draw and color some other clothes for your doll.....think about it...)

ALASKAN INDIAN DOLL AND CLOTHING

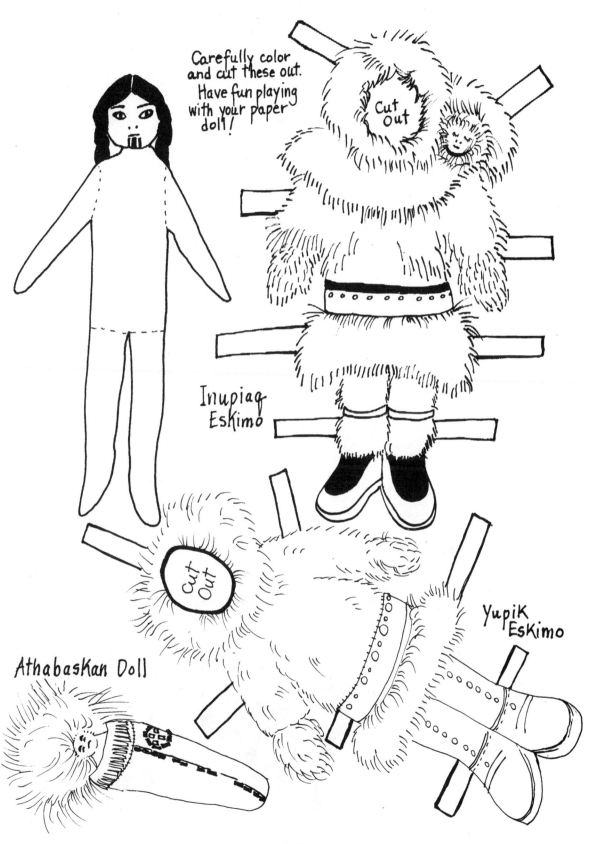

Carefully color and cut these out. Have fun playing with your paper doll!

Cut Out

Inupiaq Eskimo

Cut Out

Yupik Eskimo

Athabaskan Doll

225

Name _____

YOUR VISION QUEST IN EARLY CALIFORNIA!

You have been out in the mountains for 4 days and nights without food—or water—or sleep. Then you have a great dream! Draw here what you see. Be sure to show what animal comes to you. Show LOTS OF DETAILS.

When you finish with your drawing, write about "your experience" and explain how you felt about it.

YOUR VISION QUEST IN THE PACIFIC NORTHWEST!

You have been out in the woods for 4 days and nights without food—or water—or sleep. Then you have a great dream! Your animal helper comes to you and tells you things to help you in your life. He shows you what may happen to you in your life. Draw here what you see. Be sure to show what animal comes to you. Show LOTS OF DETAILS.

When you finish with your drawing, write about "your experience" and explain how you felt about it.

"A BEAR would be a GOOD choice!"

"A RAVEN OR an EAGLE would make a fine vision quest guide!"

"A Killer Whale would be a GREAT animal helper!"

Name ______________________________

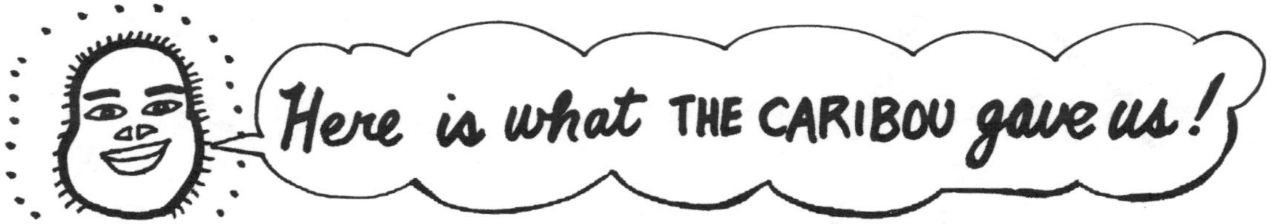

Here is what THE CARIBOU gave us!

MEAT ______________________________

HIDE ______________________________

____

____

____

____

____

BONES ______________________________

____

____

ANTLERS ______________________________

____

SINEW ______________________________

____

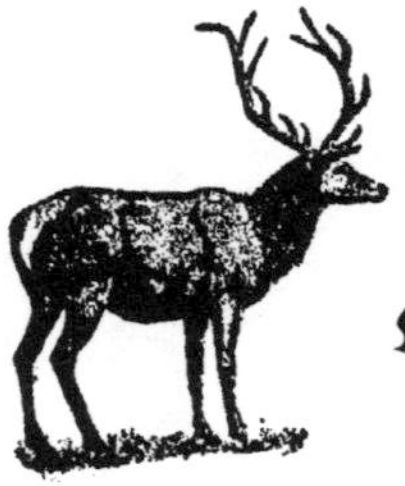

STOMACH (CONTENTS): ______________

____

TEETH ______________________________

Fill in as MANY of the blanks as you *can*.
Here are a few hints: sewing case, kayak cover, awl, wedge, whistle, drum head, dish, tool handles, spear, necklace, shoes, box, shelter, vitamins.

Name _____

Here is what THE CEDAR TREE gave the early N.W. peoples!

See how *many* objects you can list that the Northwest Indians made from cedar bark or wood. (There are at least 25 different possibilities.*)

BARK was used to make:

WOOD was used to build:

It was also used to carve:

Cedar wood was ALSO good for making:

*Think of objects they made that have to do with: food, tools, play, clothing, houses, furniture, hunting, religion, war, travel.

Here is what THE OCEAN gave the early California peoples!

Shellfish:
s _ u
b _ _
a _ _
m _ _
c _ _
o _ _
c _ _

Shells: used for _____

Sea animals: s _ _
w _ _
s _ _
e _ _

Fish: s _ _ b _ _
s _ _

Seabirds: g _ _
t _
h _
c _
p _
e _ ; eggs

Water provided: _____

Reeds, along shorelines, were used for: _____

Seaweed: used for _____

Fill in as *many* of the blanks as you can.

Here are a few hints: **Kinds of sea life:** clam, crab, cormorant, eel, salmon, tern, whale, seal, sea bass, oyster, gull, crane, abalone, pelican, heron, sea urchins, mussels, barnacles, shark (skin)

How these were used: food • mats • oil • nets • clothes • dishes • sandpaper • travel • salt • jewelry • bone digging tool • blades • sandals • doorbell! • boats • baskets

CALIFORNIA TRIBES WORD SEARCH

Look in the puzzle below and try to find the names of 21 California Indian tribes. Circle each name as you find it. The names may be written across or down (or backwards or on more than one line). GOOD LUCK!!

K	C	P	C	A	W	N	K	X	J	Y	G	W	Y
G	H	A	U	L	E	I	L	B	M	A	I	D	U
A	U	H	P	L	U	M	P	"C	I	S	N'	E	K
B	M	W	E	I	T	O	Y	I	W	P	A	"C	I
R	A	S	Ñ	U	N'	H	I	L	O	M	O	P	D
I	S	E	O	H	Y	U	R	O	K	K	N	L	O
E	H	R	P	A	S	P	K	O	Z	Q	A	I	Ñ
L	E	R	Y	"C	Y	E	R	M	U	S	T	N'	E
I	M	A	N	O	G	A	T	S	A	H	S	Z	U
N	M	S	E	L	K	O	E	D	A	Q	O	T	G
O	O	Ñ	E	S	I	U	L	N"	U	P	"C	S	E
F	J	"C	U	T	Y	K	T	I	S	T	U	Z	I
Y	A	V	E	V	S	A	L	I	N	A	N	H	D

Here are the 21 tribes to look for:

1. Cahuilla*	5. Diegueño*	9. Karok	13. Mojave	17. Shasta
2. Chumash	6. Esselen	10. Luiseño*	14. Pomo	18. Wiyot
3. Costanoan*	7. Gabrielino*	11. Maidu	15. Salina	19. Yokut
4. Cupeño*	8. Hupa	12. Miwok	16. Serrano*	20. Yuki
				21. Yurok

*Many of these so-called "Mission Indians" today are returning to ancient tribal names for their peoples.

231

PACIFIC NORTHWEST WORD SEARCH

Look in the puzzle below and try to find the 20 words that have to do with the northwest. Circle each name as you find it. The words may be written across or down (or backwards or on more than one line). GOOD LUCK!!

I	L	L	E	R	W	H	E	D	A	U	L	T	Z
K	C	H	I	L	K	A	T	U	N	Q	Y	W	S
S	E	R	C	S	E	L	E	G	I	V	D	R	A
T	C	H	L	O	N	G	H	O	U	S	E	U	L
P	L	I	B	C	A	Z	P	U	Q	V	C	D	M
O	O	N	O	O	K	S	R	T	I	X	Q	U	O
L	C	E	D	A	R	W	T	R	B	R	I	D	N
E	S	Z	S	W	Y	L	A	S	M	L	E	L	G
C	O	P	E	R	C	E	I	Y	A	K	I	M	A
L	O	P	L	Q	U	M	B	T	K	L	P	T	E
G	T	E	I	K	L	A	N	G	A	A	I	U	X
A	L	R	K	O	F	E	A	P	H	M	R	S	T
E	A	T	C	H	D	M	K	W	I	A	T	H	H

Here are the words to look for:

1. Cedar	6. Copper	11. Killer Whale	16. Oil
2. Chilkat	7. Crest Pole	12. Klamath	17. Potlatch
3. Chinook	8. Dentalium	13. Longhouse	18. Quinalt
4. Coast Salish	9. Dugout	14. Makah	19. Salmon
5. Columbia River	10. Eagle	15. Nez Perce	20. Yakima

ALASKAN WORD SEARCH

Look in the puzzle below and try to find the 19 words that have to do with Alaska. Circle each name as you find it. The words may be written across or down (or backwards or on more than one line). GOOD LUCK!!

T	K	L	T	S	I	M	S	H	I	A	N	M	A
L	M	A	I	A	T	R	W	Y	S	H	T	I	H
I	N	G	A	L	I	K	A	I	M	U	Q	H	A
N	O	E	R	G	S	A	L	E	U	T	C	S	R
G	O	S	T	O	E	Y	R	G	Q	I	A	A	P
I	P	K	S	N	O	A	U	E	L	U	R	K	O
T	R	E	G	Q	E	K	S	K	E	N	I	G	N
C	A	E	N	U	W	O	N	I	O	I	B	A	X
S	H	M	I	I	S	T	R	P	D	N	O	R	T
O	P	O	R	N	Q	U	I	U	V	E	U	D	H
R	X	S	E	A	L	S	T	Y	P	W	L	F	E
L	A	W	B	A	D	A	R	K	A	Z	G	S	S
Y	S	Y	U	P	I	A	K	U	D	O	M	I	K

Here are the 19 words to look for:

1. Aleut	6. Harpoon	11. North Eskimo	16. Walrus
2. Algonquin	7. Ingalik	12. Seal	17. Yukon
3. Badarka	8. Inuit	13. Tlingit	18. Yupiak
4. Bering Strait	9. Kashim	14. Tsimshian	19. Yupik
5. Caribou	10. Kayak	15. Umiak	

EARLY PEOPLES IN NORTH AMERICA IN 1500

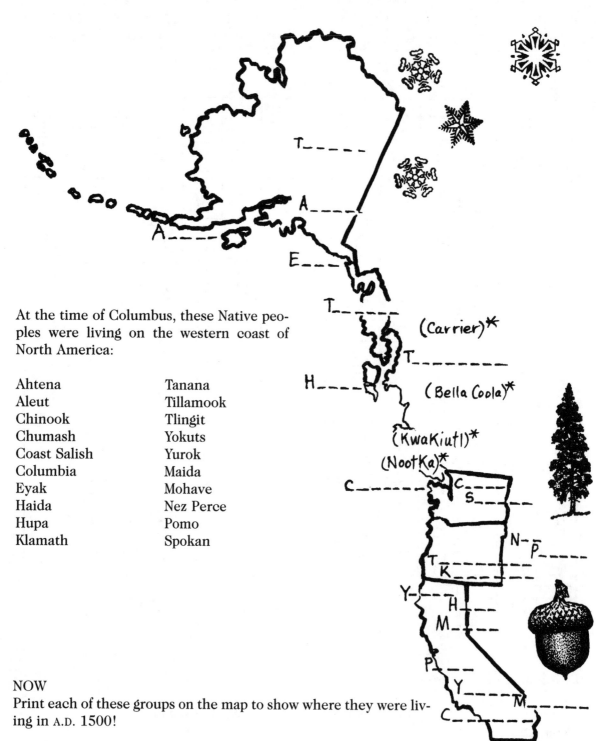

At the time of Columbus, these Native peoples were living on the western coast of North America:

Ahtena
Aleut
Chinook
Chumash
Coast Salish
Columbia
Eyak
Haida
Hupa
Klamath

Tanana
Tillamook
Tlingit
Yokuts
Yurok
Maida
Mohave
Nez Perce
Pomo
Spokan

NOW
Print each of these groups on the map to show where they were living in A.D. 1500!

*Names in parentheses are Canadian tribal groups.

© 1996 by The Center for Applied Research in Education

Name _____

PACIFIC NORTHWEST COAST TRADING

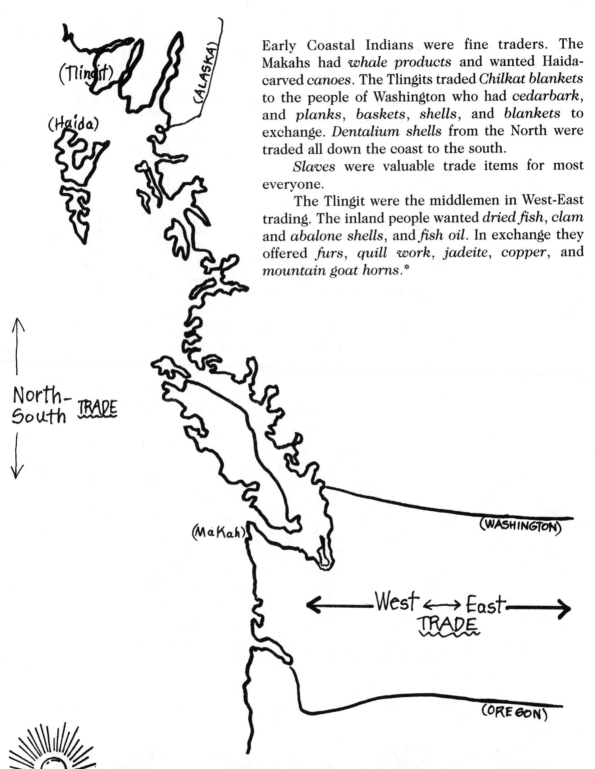

Early Coastal Indians were fine traders. The Makahs had *whale products* and wanted Haida-carved *canoes*. The Tlingits traded *Chilkat blankets* to the people of Washington who had *cedarbark*, and *planks*, *baskets*, *shells*, and *blankets* to exchange. *Dentalium shells* from the North were traded all down the coast to the south.

Slaves were valuable trade items for most everyone.

The Tlingit were the middlemen in West-East trading. The inland people wanted *dried fish*, *clam* and *abalone shells*, and *fish oil*. In exchange they offered *furs*, *quill work*, *jadeite*, *copper*, and *mountain goat horns.**

*Draw a picture of every trade item. Put it on the map to show where it first came from: a whale goes next to Makah. Color each trade item carefully.

Cut along the dotted lines on the date slips below.

Arrange the slips in order from the earliest date (top of list) to the most recent date (bottom of list). Then glue them in order along the left side of page 2. Make a small drawing or cartoon to the right of each date to go with (to illustrate) that date.

1850	California becomes a state
c. A.D. 500	Bow and arrow used in North America, replacing most atl-atls
1542	The Spaniards Cabrillo and Ferrelo explore Pacific Coast
1850-1	Mariposa War between miners and Yokuts
1812-41	Russians build Fort Ross on Pomo land in northern California
c. 10,000 B.C.	Climate changes. Ice age ends, glaciers retreat.
c. 8000 B.C.	Bering Strait replaces land bridge between continents
1869	Transcontinental railroad completed
c. 15,000 B.C. (or earlier)	Del Mar man, ancient Californian (found near Del Mar, CA)
1848-91	California Gold Rush—beginning of the end for California Indians and their way of life
1769	Portola claims California for Spain and sets up first missions with Father Serra, a Franciscan
1830	Epidemics of European diseases in California
1578-9	Sir Francis Drake explores California coast and meets Miwoks

Carefully CUT these strips apart.

In each frame draw a cartoon to illustrate one of the date strips. Keep them in the correct order.

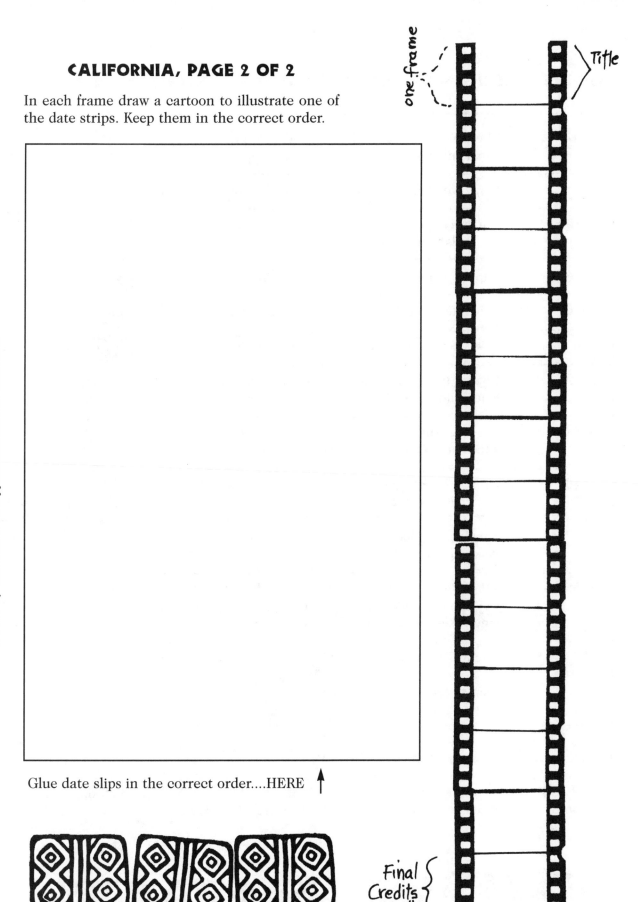

one frame

Title

Glue date slips in the correct order....HERE ↑

Final Credits (End)

1787	The N.W. ordinance called for Indian rights, tribal lands, but led to more white settlements.
c. A.D. 1	Large wooden houses in villages in Northwest
c. 5000 B.C.	Northwest people are working wood: shown by the tools found at ancient sites
1776-8	Captain Cook, English, explores Pacific Northwest
1830	Epidemics of European diseases in Oregon
1803-6	Lewis and Clark expedition to the American West
c. 500 B.C.	Copper bracelets, weapons, and amulets are made and used.
c. 5,000 B.C.	Cascade Culture people in Oregon—may be ancestors of Pacific Northwest culture
1846	Oregon country becomes part of U.S. as part of settlement with the English
1782-3	Smallpox epidemic among the Sanpoils of Washington
1855-6	Yakima War (Yakimas, Walla Wallas, Umatillas, Cayuses) in response to forced treaties and land takeovers by the U.S. government
1858	Coeur d'Alene war in Washington and Idaho (Coeur d'Alene, Spokanes, Yakimas, Paiutes): seen as second phase of Yakima wars

Carefully cut these strips apart.

Cut along the dotted lines on the date slips above.

Arrange the slips in order from the earliest date (top of list) to the most recent date (bottom of list). Then glue them in order along the left side of page 2. Make a small drawing or cartoon to the right of each date to go with (to illustrate) that date.

PACIFIC NORTHWEST, PAGE 2 OF 2

Draw a cartoon in each frame to illustrate each date. Keep them in the correct order.

one frame

Title

Glue date slips in the correct order....HERE ↑

Final Credits (End)

Cut along the dotted lines on the date slips below.

Arrange the slips in order from the earliest date (top of list) to the most recent date (bottom of list). Then glue them in order along the left side of page 2. Make a small drawing or cartoon to the right of each date to go with (to illustrate) that date.

c. 3000 B.C. to c. 1000 B.C.	Eskimo-Aleuts float across Bering Strait from Siberia and settle in Alaska
1802-1867	Tlingits drive out Russians from Sitka in 1802; they continue their resistance for 65 years
1867	U.S. buys Alaska from Russia for 7.2 million dollars
1959	Alaska becomes a state (January 3)
c. A.D. 1	Large wooden houses in villages in Alaska
c. 3000 B.C.	Ground and polished stone tools, bone tools used in Alaska
1897-1900	Klondike gold rush in Yukon: heavy traffic through Alaska
1741	Vitus Bering and Alexei Chirikof sight Alaska in July
1844	First commercial whalers in Alaska
1878	First salmon canneries in Alaska (Old Sitka and Klawok)
1843	Russians establish first mission school for Eskimos in Alaska (Greek Orthodox Church)
1799	Alexander Baranov establishes Russian post at Old Sitka
1761 - 1766	Aleuts revolt against the Russians
c. 985 - 1014	Norse (Eric the Red and Leif Ericson) make settlements in North America and meet Eskimos
c. 6000 B.C.	Alaskan campsite—shows people used stone tools, ate shellfish, seal, sea lion, deer, beaver, and blueberries

Carefully cut these strips apart.

ALASKA LIFE, PAGE 2 OF 2

Draw a cartoon in each frame to illustrate each date. Keep them in the correct order.

Glue date slips in the correct order....HERE ↑

California Cities where many Native People live TODAY

(Reno, Nevada)

S _ _ _ _ _
S _ _ _ _ _
O
S _ _ _ _ _
S _ _ _ _ _
C
S _ _ _ _ _

F _ _ _ _ _

(Las Vegas)
Nevada

L _ _ _ _ _
L _ _ _ _ _

There are 10 big cities in California where many Native Americans live today...*

Print the name of each of these cities on this map.

*1. Fresno
2. Long Beach
3. Los Angeles
4. Oakland
5. Sacramento
6. San Francisco
7. San Jose
8. Santa Clara
9. Santa Rosa
10. Stockton

Name _____

Pacific Northwest Cities where
many Native People live
TODAY

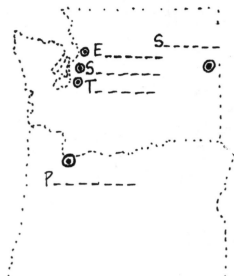

There are 5 large
North western cities
where many Native
Americans live today.
Print the name of
each of these cities
where it belongs on
this map.

1. Everett   2. Portland 3. Seattle   4. Spokane 5. Tacoma

▼▼▼▼▼▼▼ ▼▼▼▼▼▼▼ ▼▼▼▼▼▼ ▼▼▼▼▼▼▼

List 3 reasons why a Native American would want to live in
a big city:

- -

Now list 3
reasons he
or she might
Not want to
live in a big
city!

243

Name _____

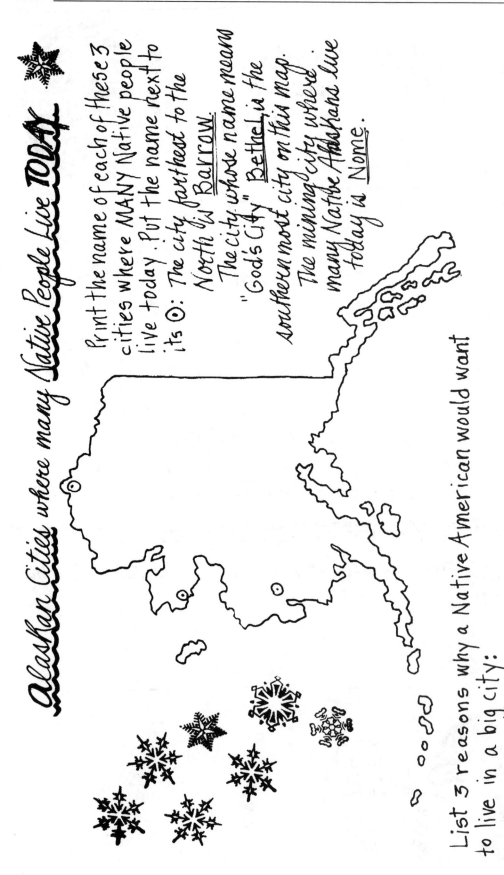

Alaskan Cities where many Native People Live TODAY

Print the name of each of these 3 cities where MANY Native people live today. Put the name next to its ⊙:

The city farthest to the North is <u>Barrow</u>.

The city whose name means "God's City" <u>Bethel</u> is the southernmost city on this map.

The mining city where many Native Alaskans live today is <u>Nome</u>.

List 3 reasons why a Native American would want to live in a big city:

What are 3 reasons a Native Alaskan might NOT want to live in a big city?

THE CALIFORNIA INDIAN RESERVATIONS AND RANCHERÍAS OF TODAY!

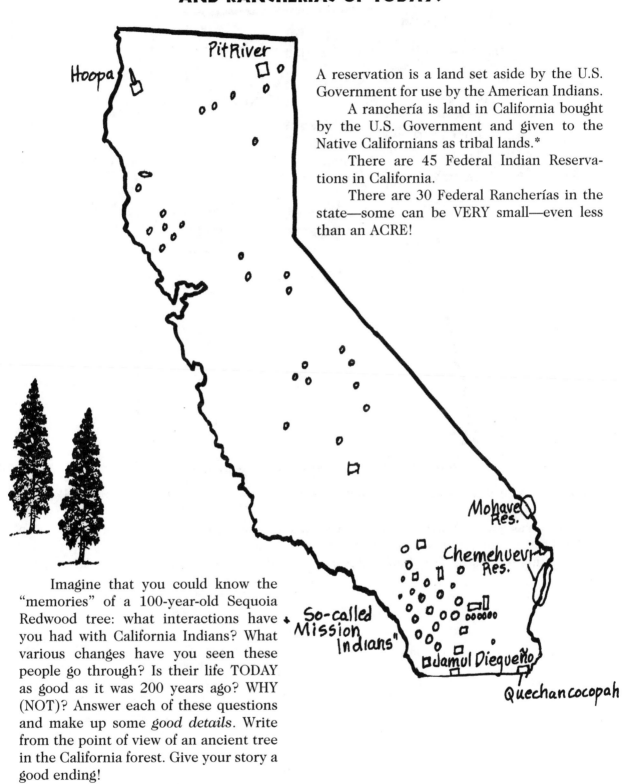

A reservation is a land set aside by the U.S. Government for use by the American Indians.

A ranchería is land in California bought by the U.S. Government and given to the Native Californians as tribal lands.*

There are 45 Federal Indian Reservations in California.

There are 30 Federal Rancherías in the state—some can be VERY small—even less than an ACRE!

Imagine that you could know the "memories" of a 100-year-old Sequoia Redwood tree: what interactions have you had with California Indians? What various changes have you seen these people go through? Is their life TODAY as good as it was 200 years ago? WHY (NOT)? Answer each of these questions and make up some *good details*. Write from the point of view of an ancient tree in the California forest. Give your story a good ending!

*Sometimes California Indians buy the ranchería land on their own.

THE FEDERAL RESERVATIONS OF WASHINGTON AND OREGON

Oregon has 3 Federal Indian Reservations: Warm Springs, Cayuse Umatilla, Burns Paiute. Print each one where it belongs on the map.

Oregon also has 1 Federal Indian Village, Celilo, a fishing site on the Washington-Oregon border. Print its name next to the **◻** on this map.

Washington has 22 U.S. Indian Reservations. Put them in alphabetical order and list them below:

1.	12.
2.	13.
3.	14.
4.	15.
5.	16.
6.	17.
7.	18.
8.	19.
9.	20.
10.	21.
11.	22.

NATIVE ALASKAN LANDS AND RESERVATIONS TODAY

1. Use a pencil to connect the dotted lines to draw the outline of Alaska.

2. Native Alaskan people are Eskimo, Aleuts, Athabaskan, (and Tsimshian). Print each of these in the part of Alaska where those native people live.*

3. There are 6 U.S. Reservations in Alaska: one is Aleut: Karluk Reservation. Color it blue. Two are *ESKIMO*: Noorvik Reservation and Elim Reservation. Color them red. Three are Athabaskan Indian Reservations: Venetie, Tetlin, and Teyonek. Color them green.

4. Annette Island is a Federal Reserve for Tsimshian Indians. Color it orange.

5. There are also *168 Eskimo villages* in ALASKA!

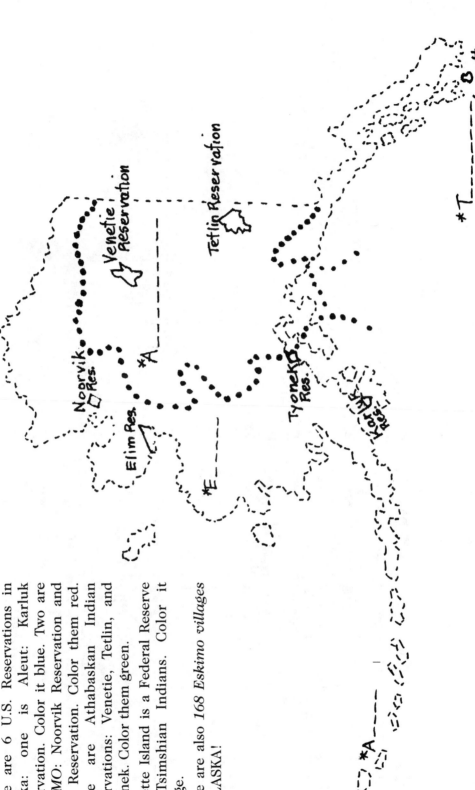

ANSWER TO EARLY CALIFORNIA INDIANS CROSSWORD PUZZLE

ANSWER TO CALIFORNIA TRIBES WORD SEARCH

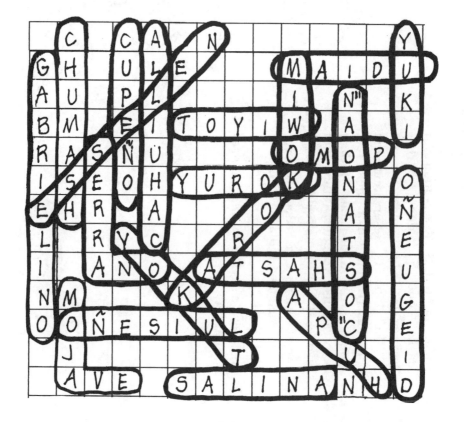

ANSWER TO NORTHWEST TRIBES WORD SEARCH

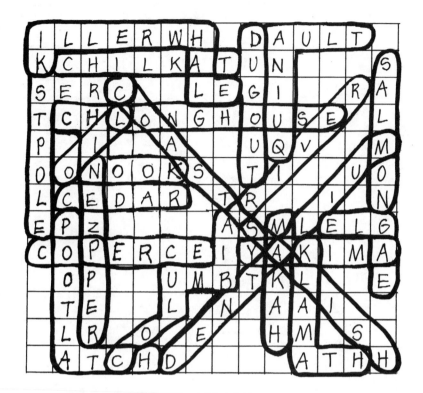

ANSWER TO ALASKAN TRIBES WORD SEARCH

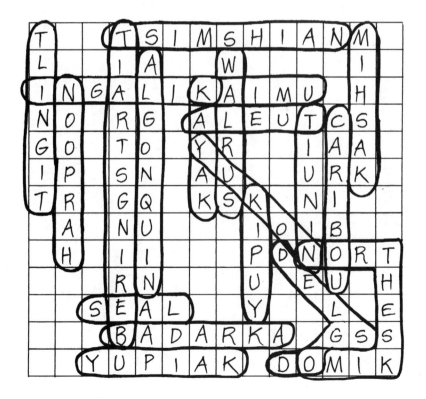

THE
COASTAL INDIANS
Teacher's Resource Guide

TEACHING MANUALS AND MATERIALS

The Teaching Store has an excellent inventory of Alaskan books, teaching manuals, puzzles, cookie cutters, etc. For a catalog and price list contact:

The Teaching Store
545 E. Northern Lights Boulevard
Anchorage, AK 99503
(907)271-7323

Primary Alaska, A Teaching Unit K-3, by Jane Niebergall, is a 65-page manual with information and activities. It, as well as other Alaska material, is available from:

Mariswood Educational Resources
Alaskan Educational Catalogue Service
Box 221955
Anchorage, AK 99522

Smithsonian Resource Guide for Teachers is free. Material from The National Museum of the American Indian is listed in this catalog, which can be ordered from:

Office of Elementary and Secondary Education
Smithsonian Institution
Arts and Industries Building
Room 1163, MRC 402
Washington, D.C. 20560

Before ordering any materials, please check with the Museum for availability. Call (202)357-2425.

The Burke Museum covers the natural and cultural history of the Pacific Rim; its Gift Shop offers materials on Northwest Coast Native arts and culture including activity books, postcards, posters, videos, music, and sets of slides. (*Slide set No. 5* is excellent: 25 images from the Pacific Northwest, $17.55.) The Gift Shop phone number is (206)685-0909 and its FAX is 206-685-3039. For the museum's Educator's Retail Catalog write to:

Burke Museum
University of Washington
Box 353010
Seattle, WA 98195-3010

Daybreak Star Cultural and Educational Foundation offers excellent inexpensive teaching materials concerning (Pacific Northwest) Native peoples, including:

Sharing Our Worlds
Native American Children Today

Contemporary Northwest Native American children speak of their lives in first-person accounts. These materials include lots of black-and-white photos in a 30-page spiral-bound format. Other titles are:

Squamish Today (good black-and-white photos)
Mamook Book K-4 (activities for learning about Northwest Indians; excellent large format)

For information about availability and latest prices, call 206-285-4425 or write to:

United Indians of All Tribes Foundation
Daybreak Star Cultural and Educational Center
Discovery Park
P.O. Box 99100
Seattle, WA 98199

BOOKS

The Columbus Encounter—A Multicultural View explores the Columbus controversy and the meaning of culture. It takes a look at the Americas' early people and visitors. For the current price and ordering information, contact:

Zephyr Press
3316 N. Chapel Avenue
P.O. Box 66006-LA
Tucson, AZ 85728-6006
(520)322-5090

California Reference Books

Keeping Slug Woman Alive (California Indian Texts)
Mabel McKay, Weaving the Dream (Biography of a Pomo woman)

These books, as well as a catalog of new and selected texts (including American Indian Studies,) are available from The University of California Press. For prices and ordering information, contact:

The University of California Press
2120 Berkeley Way
Berkeley, CA 94720

Native Ways, California Indian Stories and Memories, edited by Malcolm Margolin and Yolanda Montijo, was published in 1995. Contact:

Heyday Books
P.O. Box 9145
Berkeley, CA 94709
(510)549-3564

Chumash, a Picture of Their World by Bruce Miller is available from:

Sand River Press
1319 14th Street
Los Osos, CA 93402

Pacific Northwest Reference Books

Indian Legends of the Pacific Northwest is available from The University of California Press
The Coast Salish Peoples
The Chinook
The Yakima

These books are published by:

Chelsea House Publishers
300 Park Avenue South
New York, NY 10010-5313

Their *Indians of North America Series* includes within its seventy volumes books on the California Indians and the Inuit.

Alaska Reference Books

The Native People of Alaska by Steve J. Langdon is published by:

Greatland Graphics
Anchorage, AK 99522

Make Prayers to the Raven, a Koyukon View of the Northern Forest by Richard K. Nelson is a 300-page scholarly text sprinkled with Alaskan Native riddles. The paperback edition published in 1986 is available from:

The University of Chicago Press
11030 S. Langley Avenue
Chicago, IL 60628

MAGAZINES

Skipping Stones, a Multi-cultural Children's Quarterly is a timely, timeless resource for multicultural and nature awareness. (Back issues are available for $5 each.)

Focus on Native Societies of the Americas, vol. 4, no. 3, and vol. 6, no. 4.
Indigenous Societies/Rainforest, vol. 4, no. 4.

Skipping Stones Magazine
P.O. Box 3939
Eugene, OR 97403-0939
(541)342-4956

Cobblestone: The History Magazine for Young Children offers a rich variety of information, addresses, and illustrations. The following back issues contain articles of interest to teachers of older students:

The Legacy of Columbus, 1992, no. 1
California History, 1985, no. 5
Yukon Gold Rush, 1980, no. 8
Lewis and Clark, 1980, no. 9
Whaling, 1984, no. 4
Transcontinental Railroad, 1980, no. 5
Oregon Trail, 1981, no. 12
Indians of the Northwest, 1992, no. 11

For information on subscriptions and back issues, call toll free 1-800-821-0115.

Cobblestone Publishing Inc.
7 School Street
Petersborough, NH 03458-1454

News from Native California
This journal publishes serious, highly readable and entertaining articles that can be enjoyed by sixth to eighth graders.

News from Native California
Box 9145
Berkeley, CA 94709
(415)848-3423

Also available from this publisher is the 45-page booklet *Peek-Wa Stories*, originally published as *Ancient Indian Legends of California*. The stories were collected in 1938 by Karuk scholar Grover C. Sanderson and have been updated by his son, Jack Sanderson, Sr.

Native Peoples

This is a sleek magazine with high color photos (and ads). It covers a wide variety of contemporary and historical Native American topics. Each issue comes with a 20-page Study Guide that has reproducibles.

Native Peoples Magazine
P.O. Box 36820
Phoenix, AZ 85067-6820
(602)252-2236

MAPS

The National Geographic Society publishes fine maps (on heavy-coated paper) including *Close Up USA No. 14—Alaska*. For the complete map list, write to:

National Geographic Society
1145 17th Street, NW
Washington, D.C. 20036

Alaska Official State Map
Have a student write for a free map to:

Alaska Division of Tourism
P.O. Box 110801
Juneau, AK 99811-0801

VIDEOS

Chumash Indian Rock Art—usually not accessible to the public—is documented in a VHS cassette #405 *Mountain Parks in Los Angeles*. Order from:

The Ecology Center of Southern California
P.O. Box 35473
Los Angeles, CA 90035
(213)559-5160

Indian America: A Gift from the Past
The Makah tell the story of what the Ozette discoveries mean to them and how the excavation changed their lives. To order and for information, call toll free 1-800-775-FILM.

AUDIOTAPES

Stories from the Spirit World: Myths and Legends of Native America is a series of eight half-hour programs (focused on Cahuilla and Chumash Indians of California and the Aztecs of Pre-Columbian Mexico) that were aired on National Public Radio in the late 1980s. It includes field recordings and dramatizations of eyewitness accounts of the original encounter with the Spanish explorers, all recreated by Native American performers. To order, call toll free 1-800-253-0808, or write to:

NPR Cassettes
P.O. Box 55417
Madison, WI 53705

REPLICAS

Craig Bates, who works for the Forest Service in Yosemite National Park, makes handsome replications of early Native American tools, toys, and utensils. Mr. Bates is not Native American, but he has decades of personal contact with California native peoples and his respect for their history is clear in the craftsmanship of his pieces. He will make replicas of wooden, stone, leather, or grass articles. (His acorn tops and mortar and pestles are great favorites with the children who come to the Jesse Peter Native American Art Museum in Santa Rosa, California.)

His pieces cost from fifty cents to $1,000, depending on size and the time required to make them. He usually has orders two to three months in advance, so it is best to call or Fax ahead to make inquiries. The numbers are: FAX 209-372-0458, WORK (209)379-2318, and HOME (209)372-0282. Or write to:

Craig Bates
P.O. Box 577
Yosemite, CA 95389